Dual Language
EDUCATION

Dual Language
EDUCATION

Program Design and Implementation

Sonia W. Soltero

HEINEMANN
Portsmouth, NH

Heinemann
361 Hanover Street
Portsmouth, NH 03801–3912
www.heinemann.com

Offices and agents throughout the world

The author and publisher wish to thank those who have generously given permission to reprint borrowed material:

Inter-American Magnet School Mission Statement reprinted with permission from the Inter-American Magnet School, Chicago, Illinois. All rights reserved.

Cummins' Dual Iceberg Image adapted from *ESL Teaching: Principles for Success*, Revised Edition, by Yvonne Freeman, David Freeman, Mary Soto, and Ann Ebe. Copyright © 2016, 1998 by Yvonne Freeman, David Freeman, Mary Soto, and Ann Ebe. Published by Heinemann, Portsmouth, NH. All rights reserved.

Image credits: page 70 © Alamy/HIP; page 79 © V. Yakobchuk/Fotolia/HIP; page 110 © Arto/Fotolia/HIP

Library of Congress Cataloging-in-Publication Data
Names: Soltero, Sonia W.
Title: Dual language education : program design and implementation / Sonia W. Soltero.
Description: Portsmouth, NH : Heinemann, 2016. | Includes bibliographical references and index.
Identifiers: LCCN 2016028090 | ISBN 9780325078137
Subjects: LCSH: Education, Bilingual—United States.
Classification: LCC LC3731 .S6654 2016 | DDC 370.117—dc23
LC record available at https://lccn.loc.gov/2016028090

Editor: Holly Kim Price
Production: Victoria Merecki
Cover design: Suzanne Heiser
Interior design: Shawn Girsberger
Typesetter: Shawn Girsberger
Manufacturing: Steve Bernier

Printed in the United States of America on acid-free paper
3 4 5 6 7 RWP 23 22 21 20
July 2020 Printing

To my parents,

Patricia and Peter,

for your love and support,

and for giving me the gift of

a bilingual education.

Without the wonderful opportunities

you gave me,

none of what I have accomplished

would have been possible.

CONTENTS

ACKNOWLEDGMENTS

Many people contributed to this book in both direct and indirect ways. My heartfelt and deep appreciation to all those who supported, inspired, and motivated me to complete this book. My infinite gratitude to José for always encouraging and supporting me to continue to grow and follow my lifelong passion for promoting bilingual education. Muchas gracias go to my dear friend Sharon Spellman for your invaluable insights, advice, and support. And to Alexa Lil, thank you for letting me in the wondrous world of a simultaneous bilingual child.

In my many years in the dual language education field, I have worked with countless numbers of dedicated and passionate educators and policy makers who, in spite of an entrenched anti-bilingual climate, have fiercely advocated for and improved the education of language learners. Because of limitation in space I cannot thank them all, so I mention just a few with whom I have worked and who stand out because of their tireless advocacy of, enduring devotion for, and fearless defense of bilingual education: Tomasita Ortiz, Frances Rivera, Martine Santos, Jason Goulah, Karen Garibay-Mulattieri, Claudia Solano, Elizabeth Cardenas-Lopez, Reyna Hernandez, and Josie Yanguas. I would also like to acknowledge the many school and district leaders who, in spite of so many obstacles and challenges, have advanced dual language programs in their schools. An especially well-deserved thank-you to the school leaders who make up the Chicago Public School Dual Language Principal Consortium: Tony Acevedo, Olimpia Bahena, Frances Garcia, Ted Johnson, Javier Arriola-Lopez, Diego Giraldo, Stacy Steward, Estuardo Mazin, Tamara, Witzl, Judi Sauri, Renee Mackin, and Gwen Kasper-Couty. I have been lucky to work with so many who have dedicated their lives to educating and advocating for bilingual learners. A very special thank-you to Yvonne and David Freeman for your continued support and friendship. And thank you, Gila Rivera, for sharing your enthusiasm about bilingual education and the inspiring quote that opens this book. My gratitude to all the teachers, school leaders, students, and families who believe in dual language education and advocate for additive bilingual education. ✳

INTRODUCTION

Make the strangers welcome in this land, let them keep their languages and customs, for weak and fragile is the realm which is based on a single language or on a single set of customs.

—St. Stephen, first King of Hungary, in a letter to his son St. Eneric, 1036 AD

When her principal began talking about starting a two-way dual language program, Alexa thought, "Here we go again, jumping on the bandwagon of the latest fad. Don't we already have enough on our plate?" She was not the only teacher in the school who was growing tired of what seemed like a never-ending revolving door of new programs and initiatives that they had to invest time and energy in learning about and aligning to their curriculum and instruction. Alexa, a well-respected and dedicated teacher, had taught in the transitional bilingual program at Recoleta Elementary School for more than seventeen years. Alexa's original negative reaction came from years of implementing new programs imposed from district and school administrators, only to be abandoned a few years later. She thought they did not need to embark on yet another short-lived "experiment" and made this abundantly clear to the other teachers, parents, and the principal whenever she had the opportunity. But after months of discussions, the majority of the teachers, support staff, and parents voted in favor of implementing a dual language program at Recoleta. Even though she would not technically have to teach in the program for a few years, she made it known that when dual language reached fourth grade, she would move to the middle school grades to avoid teaching in the program.

Unexpectedly, by the time dual language reached fourth grade, Alexa was one of the program's most enthusiastic and committed supporters. What made her change her mind so drastically? During the planning phase and the first year of implementation, Alexa began to hear about dual language education from the prekindergarten (PK) and kindergarten teachers and from parents of children who had participated in the program that first year. She slowly became interested in learning more about dual language and realized that maybe this new initiative would not just be a passing fad like all the others had been. She began to understand that many of the premises on which dual language is based very much aligned with her own views about developing bilingualism and bilingual teaching approaches. Years later, Alexa shared that her change of heart was partly because she felt free to express her opinion and ask questions. She also thought that this time the decision-making process was more collaborative, and there was a more comprehensive "fact-finding" effort and a well-thought-out planning process. Alexa saw firsthand how students in the dual language program were progressing academically in their first and second languages. She also often heard how happy parents were with their children's participation in the program. What impressed her most were the friendships and interactions that had developed between English learners (ELs) and native English-speaking students, bilingual and general education teachers, and families from the two language groups. This was something that seldom happened before the dual language program was implemented. EL families and their teachers had little interaction with students and families from the general education classrooms, so it was a welcomed and unexpected surprise for Alexa that this was happening. This segregation was slowly giving way to meaningful collaborations and friendships across languages and cultures at Recoleta.

The transformation that Alexa experienced illustrates the types of positive outcomes that come from developing comprehensive understandings about dual language education and the many possibilities and opportunities it affords when well-designed and implemented. This book provides guidelines and research-based evidence to build the comprehensive knowledge necessary to plan and implement sustainable high-quality dual language programs.

I write this book from the lens of a practitioner, not just an outsider researcher. My background and experiences as a dual language public school teacher for fourteen years and dual language program coordinator give me an unusual insider viewpoint and understanding about what it takes to create effective, long-lasting dual language programs. Because I am also a product of dual language education, I have firsthand experience of what it is like to be a dual language student in K–12 schools. This book is based on my thirty years in the field of bilingual education as a dual language teacher, dual language program coordinator, researcher, and professional developer. The focus of my research over the past decades has been on dual language program design and curricular development, as well as leadership practices in program implementation, sustainability, and improvement.

This book is intended for teachers, school leaders, and district administrators interested in implementing new dual language programs, as well as those looking to improve their existing models. Each chapter examines the pedagogical and organizational principles of dual language education and the specific conditions and features necessary for their effective implementation and sustainability. Included are in-depth discussions on fundamental elements that must be considered when

[Handwritten margin notes:]
Alexa was able to express her opinion and ask questions.

① Lago Agrio
② TAXi a la frontera
③ La punta puente... (cuento color)
④ La Hormiga.
⑤ Villagarzon

I like the fact — the author writes the book from the perspective of all education, not just doing research without experiency

hands on / first hand to mistakes / self correction / or inventory which are extreanly important to pedagogy.

putting dual language education into practice, as well as challenges that often arise while developing and implementing dual language programs.

Without a doubt, current demographic changes in the PK–12 student population present many challenges for educators, while at the same time offer exciting new opportunities to implement innovative and forward-thinking additive language programs that benefit all students alike. In the last few years, there has been a resurgence of interest in dual language education from policy makers, educators, and parents. Several states have launched statewide initiatives to grow and implement dual language programs, including Utah, Delaware, Rhode Island, and North Carolina. The Seal of Biliteracy, legislated into law in a number of states, points to a collective desire to celebrate and embrace multilingualism in the United States. The Seal of Biliteracy was first passed by the California legislature in 2011, followed by New York in 2012, and Illinois in 2014. Currently twenty-one states, plus the District of Columbia, have passed legislation making the Seal of Biliteracy state law, and thirteen others are developing legislation.

Another positive trend has been the sudden increase in universities and colleges offering dual language coursework and special certificates. Teacher-preparation programs across the United States are offering this specialized coursework in response to school districts' needs for better-prepared dual language teachers and school leaders. Currently, universities and colleges that offer coursework on dual language education include San Diego State University, University of Minnesota, Webster State University, Bank Street College, California State University Long Beach, University of Texas at Arlington, University of Saint Thomas, Brigham Young University, Utah State University. These statewide initiatives and teacher-preparation trends, coupled with a growing thaw on restrictions of bilingual education in several states (most notably the current movement in California to overturn Proposition 227, which banned bilingual education), indicate strong leanings toward acceptance and promotion of bilingual education for all. Shin (2013) argues that "creating a 'language competent' society requires a concerted effort of educators, policymakers, families and communities. As a society, we need to realize that the languages spoken by ethnic and linguistic minorities are a national asset, a resource that must not be wasted. Students who come from homes where languages other than English are spoken should be supported to maintain those languages while learning English. And students who speak English natively should be supported to learn another language" (95).

About This Book

Because the majority of dual language programs are in PK–6 schools, many of the examples, considerations, and recommendations in this book have an elementary

Handwritten margin notes:
laws of bilingual education.
demographic = relating to the structure of populations:
"The demographic trend is toward an older population."
2016 — book published
Bilingual education continues to be popular often: xenophobia in the United States coming from both political parties!

school lens. While most of the suggestions and examples also apply to middle and high school settings, differences in planning and implementation are discussed throughout the book, accompanied by examples that speak specifically to these grade bands, particularly for scheduling. Many of the premises and guidelines presented here also apply to transitional bilingual education, especially late-exit programs. This book is intended primarily for the United States context, but the topics are also relevant to dual language and additive bilingual programs in other countries where two languages are part of the educational curriculum. Each chapter includes real-life narratives from teachers, parents, and school leaders as they reflect on their experiences planning and implementing their programs—all names have been changed to maintain confidentiality.

Chapter 1 introduces the theoretical and research premises, as well as the foundational structures of dual language education. **Chapter 2** explains the planning process and steps for designing comprehensive, sustainable, and high-quality programs. **Chapter 3** elaborates on key programmatic components and processes in the first few years of implementation that build on program planning discussed in the previous chapters. **Chapter 4** focuses on various aspects of bilingualism, the relationship between the first and second language in the context of teaching and learning, as well as current research findings on the neurological and cognitive advantages of bilingualism as a foundation for expanded bilingual and biliterate skills. **Chapter 5** describes the types of instructional and assessment practices that are best suited for dual language classrooms that optimize bilingual learners' academic and biliterate development. In **Chapter 6**, the focus is twofold: culturally responsive schoolwide practices and supportive leadership practices. The two appendices at the end of the book offer a variety of resources for dual language teachers, school leaders, and families: **Appendix A** includes a glossary of terms used in the field of dual language education; **Appendix B** provides a comprehensive list of resources, including professional organizations, information and research centers, national education conferences, instructional materials catalogs, films and videos, and Internet sites and blogs.

This book offers a comprehensive view of what it takes to create well-designed, effective, and sustainable dual language programs. The recommendations for planning, implementation, improvement, and evaluation are based on dual language research and theoretical foundations. The quote at the beginning of this introduction speaks to the inclusive nature of dual language education and the need to embrace the multiple languages and cultures that are the common realities of most countries around the world, including the United States. Almost a thousand years ago, the King of Hungary made the powerful statement to his son, who was soon to be the next king. As you read through this book, keep in mind the words spoken by the

King of Hungary as the most fundamental premise that drives us to create and implement dual language programs, reflected in a more current quote that follows.

> *The very act of acquiring knowledge and linguistic competence has a positive disproportional impact on the economic potential of an individual. Furthermore it contributes to the likelihood that the individual can make a greater contribution to his/her society. Quite literally their capacity to participate in their society is considerably enhanced . . . But in a society where there are large linguistic minorities, failure to promote equal treatment of the language of the minority involves losing the contribution that the minority group can make to the overall value added in the human capital or knowledge-based sector.* (Chorney 1997, 181) ✳

Dual Language Education Foundations

The United States has the unique opportunity to be at the forefront of a more visionary, but also a more practical language policy. The nation is host to most of the world's languages due to trends in immigration flow. In fact, the three most spoken languages in the US are also the three most spoken languages in the world: English, Spanish and Chinese. The US is poised to take the lead in the global marketplace, but to do so, it must first acknowledge the tremendous, unique resource that exists within its cultural and linguistic diversity. . . . Clearly, it is time for American educators to realize that English-only instruction is a vestige of another era and the new economy calls for a multilingual approach to educating America's children.

—Patricia C. Gándara and Rebecca M. Callahan, "Looking Toward the Future"

why U.S. is important in the field of Bilingual Education.

Bilingualism and bilingual education are increasing around the world. In large part this is because of the rise in global digital communication, increase of international travel and commerce, and growing migration. Grosjean (2010) reports that an estimated half of the world's population is bilingual. This boost in multilingualism is also a result of more people around the world choosing to educate their children in a second language (L2), particularly in English, Spanish, Chinese, and Arabic. Baker (2011) suggests that "the ownership of two or more languages is increasingly seen as an asset as the 'communication world' gets smaller" (411).

No doubt, English has become the global *lingua franca* (or preferred language), not only because it is seen as a language of status, but also because it is a language widely used for international commerce and technology. Unfortunately, the global enthusiasm for acquiring English has promoted monolingualism among native English speakers, sometimes resulting in negative attitudes toward learning other languages (García 2009). This view about bilingualism is felt in the general indifference for learning foreign languages in schools and universities and the continued efforts to eliminate bilingual education for ELs. Because dual language programs develop academic, linguistic, social, and cross-cultural competencies, they have the potential to counter these negative perceptions and provide opportunities for *all* students to become bilingual, biliterate, and transcultural.

[handwritten margin note: more than half of student population are bilingual ||| parent are now choosing to raised their children in a]

[handwritten note: → English speakers, don't want to learn english as the result of English lingua franca.]

Foundational Structures of Dual Language Education

The highest possible academic, linguistic, and sociocultural outcomes for bilingual learners rest on the strength of the foundations of the dual language program, which must be based on theory and research as well as sound educational practices. This foundation serves as the platform for the three pillars of dual language education (see Figure 1-1): (1) committed, knowledgeable, and well-prepared teachers and school leaders; (2) culturally and linguistically responsive instruction, curriculum, and assessment; and (3) engaged and supportive families and community. These pillars, in turn, support the development of academically successful, bilingual, biliterate, and cross-cultural students.

Dual Language Program Features and Goals

In general, the various models that use two languages for content instruction fall under the umbrella of bilingual education even though researchers and educators differ on the various terms and definitions that are used in the field. For example, some consider late-exit transitional bilingual education to be a developmental model, while others regard two-way bilingual education and dual language as different programs. For the purpose of this book, the term *dual language*, also known as *bilingual immersion* and *two-way immersion*, is defined as follows (see Figure 1-2).

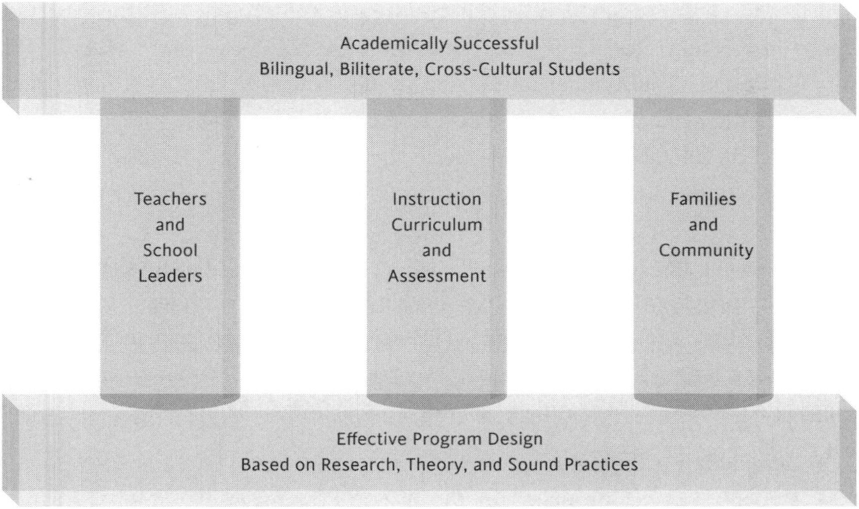

FIGURE **1-1**
Foundational Structures of
Dual Language Education

Academically Successful
Bilingual, Biliterate, Cross-Cultural Students

Teachers
and
School
Leaders

Instruction
Curriculum
and
Assessment

Families
and
Community

Effective Program Design
Based on Research, Theory, and Sound Practices

The term *immersion* sometimes causes confusion among educators and policy makers, who might think that dual language immersion programs are intended to immerse English speakers in the language other than English (LOTE) and ELs in English. A public school district whose Board of Trustees recently decided not to expand their dual language program into middle school argued that Spanish-speaking students should be immersed in English classrooms and English-speaking students in Spanish classrooms. Canadian immersion programs are often cited when making this type of argument in favor of immersing ELs in English, without understanding that in the United States the outcomes and contexts are entirely different than in Canada (Baker 2011; Cummins 2001; de Jong 2011). In the additive Canadian bilingual model, the goal is bilingualism and biliteracy, the two languages hold equal status in the country, teachers are bilingual in French and English, instruction is in both languages, and the parents choose to enroll their children in the program. On the other hand, in the subtractive structure English immersion model of the United States, the goal is monolingualism in English, the LOTE has a lower status to English, teachers are mostly English monolingual speakers, instruction is only in

FIGURE **1-2**
Definition of Dual
Language Education

Dual language education is a long-term additive bilingual and cross-cultural program model that consistently uses two languages for content instruction, learning, and communication, where students develop high levels of bilingual, biliterate, academic, and cross-cultural competencies.

English, and parents must enroll their children in the program. In the structured English immersion model, students' first language (L1) is replaced with English, while in the French-Canadian immersion model, students' English is not replaced but rather enhanced after they have acquired French as their L2. It is important to understand and be able to articulate these significant differences between additive (Canadian bilingual immersion) and subtractive (United States English immersion) models.

All dual language programs use at least two languages for teaching and learning content areas, literacy, and culture. In the United States, the typical dual language program is offered in English and a LOTE—most commonly Spanish, but increasingly in other languages like Chinese, Arabic, and French. Dual language programs are designed for a variety of student populations that include:

- bilingual or trilingual students
- students not yet proficient in the primary language of school (ELs in the United States or non-Norwegian speakers in Norway)
- students proficient in the primary language of school (English speakers in the United States or Spanish speakers in Guatemala)
- students who no longer speak their heritage language (Korean-descent students in Argentina or Japanese-descent students in Brazil)
- students who speak an indigenous language or who no longer speak the heritage language (Navajo in the United States or Nahuatl in Mexico).

Dual language is most common in elementary schools, but programs in middle and high schools are on the rise, and all are driven by three universal goals: bilingualism and biliteracy, high academic achievement, and cross-cultural competencies (see Figure 1-3).

Developing full proficiency in academic and conversational language in two languages is the principal goal of dual language education. What distinguishes dual language from other programs is that bilingual and biliterate skills are achieved by learning the L2 through the content areas over an extended period of time. Because effective dual language programs are closely aligned to national and state learning standards, students are expected to achieve academically at or above grade level in all content areas in both languages. Cross-cultural competency is also a major goal that aims to expand students' multicultural perspectives, intergroup skills, and positive self-image (Soltero 2004). The most effective programs do not just focus on bilingual and biliterate skills, but also build transcultural knowledge and

FIGURE **1-3**
Dual Language Education
Goals

Bilingualism and Biliteracy → High Academic Achievement → Cross-Cultural Competencies

cross-cultural identities (Lindholm-Leary 2012). Unfortunately, in an attempt to fit an ever-expanding curriculum into what seems a shrinking school day, cross-cultural competencies and multicultural knowledge are often left out of students' learning experiences. This cross-cultural component is essential in dual language programs because a new language cannot be fully acquired without learning about its cultures. Cultural affirmation is particularly important for ELs because they come from families that often experience marginalization and stereotyping. Developing cross-cultural competencies must go beyond the typical "heroes and holidays" approach (Lee, Menkart, and Okazawa-Rey 2007) that occasionally celebrates people and events from nondominant groups, such as Cinco de Mayo or Chinese New Year. Cross-cultural competencies must also include deeper understandings of the intersection between cultural aspects of the LOTE and English. The integration of LOTE speakers' cultural background in the curriculum, culturally appropriate instructional practices for ELs, authentic instructional materials, and nonbiased assessments best support dual language cross-cultural goals.

great point about cross-cultural competencies.

Demographic Realities and Shifting Mindsets

There is no denying that the student makeup of today's classrooms is increasingly diverse. The National Center for Education Statistics (2015) reports that for the first time, the number of Latino, Asian, and African American students in PK–12 schools in the United States has exceeded that of White non-Latino students. This growth is due to increases in Latino and Asian student populations, many coming from homes where a LOTE is spoken. Fourteen states, plus the District of Columbia, already have majority-minority student populations and several are on the verge of becoming majority-minority, including Alaska, North Carolina, and Illinois. Gándara and Callahan (2014) note how different the experiences of today's minority youth are to those of past generations: "Children of immigrants today are coming of age in a majority-minority era" (294).

The number of ELs in PK–12 classrooms has increased by sixty percent in the last decade, compared with a seven-percent growth of the general student population. In 2013, ELs made up almost eleven percent of the total student population, with 5.3 million enrolled in K–12 schools. By 2020, estimates indicate that half of all public school students will come from non-English-speaking backgrounds (National Center for Education Statistics 2015). The states with the largest numbers of ELs now include Rhode Island, Connecticut, and Massachusetts (see Figure 1-4). EL enrollments have increased dramatically in states where the majority of students traditionally had spoken only English. This growth ranges from 135 percent in North Carolina to 610 percent in South Carolina. The top ten states with the largest growth in ELs are mostly in the Southeastern part of the country: Kentucky, Nevada,

FIGURE **1-4**
States with the Largest Share of ELs (2013)

California	45%
New Mexico	36%
Texas	35%
New Jersey	30%
Nevada	30%
New York	30%
Florida	27%
Arizona	27%
Hawaii	25%
Illinois	23%
Massachusetts	22%
Connecticut	22%
Rhode Island	21%

Delaware, Arkansas, Kansas, Mississippi, Alabama, Virginia, North Carolina, and South Carolina.

Even though there are over 150 languages spoken by school-age ELs, Spanish has the highest number of speakers (seventy-one percent), followed by Chinese (four percent), Vietnamese (three percent), French/Haitian Creole (two percent), and Arabic (two percent) (Ryan 2013). Latino-origin ELs represent almost half of all Latino students in schools. Because Spanish is so widely spoken in the United States, this book provides many examples of Spanish-English dual language programs. However, these examples can be applied to programs that use languages other than Spanish. Camarota and Zeigler (2014) report that the number of people who speak a language other than English at home "reached an all-time high of 61.8 million, up 2.2 million since 2010. The largest increases from 2010 to 2013 were for speakers of Spanish, Chinese, and Arabic. One in five U.S. residents now speaks a foreign language at home" (1). The demographic realities of the United States related to Latino and Chinese populations are especially noteworthy. After English and Spanish, Chinese is the most spoken language in this country. The continual growth of Latino Spanish speakers, as well as Chinese and Arabic speakers in the United States points to the marketability of having academic and professional competencies in English plus additional languages. Between 1990 and 2013, the Latino population grew faster than any other ethnic or racial group and is projected to be almost one-third of the total population by 2050. Census data (Census Bureau 2010) also show nearly three million people spoke Chinese in the United States in 2011, a 360 percent increase from 1980. Camarota and Zeigler report that LOTE speakers increased to 2.2 million between 2010 and 2013, a thirty-two percent growth since 2000 and ninety-four percent growth since 1990 (see Figure 1-5).

FIGURE **1-5**
Largest Increases in LOTE Speakers in the U.S., 2010–2013

The largest increases from 2010 to 2013 were speakers of:
- Spanish (up 1.4 million, 4 percent growth)
- Chinese (up 220,000, 8 percent growth)
- Arabic (up 188,000, 22 percent growth)
- Urdu (up 50,000, 13 percent growth)

LOTEs with more than one million speakers in 2013:
- Spanish (38.4 million)
- Chinese (3 million)
- Tagalog (1.6 million)
- Vietnamese (1.4 million)
- French (1.3 million)
- Korean (1.1 million)
- Arabic (1.1 million)

Making the Case for Dual Language Programs

In one form or another, bilingual education has been offered in the United States since the 1600s, with alternating periods that either embraced or rejected it. After a long period of suppression, bilingual education was restored in the early 1960s by Cuban exiles in Dade County, Florida. Recognizing the importance of educating their children in Spanish and English, families established the first dual language program at Coral Way Elementary School in 1963, which is still in existence more than fifty years later and today is known as the Coral Way Bilingual K–8 Center. Dual language education is not a new idea—Canada, India, Sweden, Switzerland, and China, among other countries, have successfully implemented this form of additive bilingual and multilingual education for decades.

Dual language education capitalizes on the rich linguistic assets reflected in communities across the United States and also responds to the need for a biliterate and transcultural workforce. Market analysts point to the increasing need for bilingual, biliterate, and cross-cultural professionals in the United States and abroad. Having multiliterate citizens enhances intercultural competences, intergroup relations, and global economic competitiveness. For instance, the National Security Language Initiative for Youth promotes national efforts to expand critical world language education in K–16 and aims to prepare "leaders in a global world. Now more than ever, it is essential that Americans have the necessary linguistic skills and cultural knowledge to promote international dialogue and support American engagement abroad. NSLI-Y aims to provide opportunities to American youth that will spark a lifetime interest in language learning."

More significantly, the achievement gap for ELs is best addressed through high-quality additive programs where their language and culture are not only valued, but also promoted and developed. According to the 2013 National Assessment of Educational Progress (National Center for Education Statistics 2015), the average scores for ELs in reading assessment in fourth, eighth, and twelfth grades were significantly lower than the average score for non-ELs. The National Center for Education Statistics (2015) reported that reading score gaps widened by grade, from thirty-nine points in fourth grade, to forty-five points in eighth grade, and to fifty-three points in twelfth grade. For math NAEP assessment average scores in the same grades, the gap between ELs and non-ELs widened from twenty-five points in fourth grade, to forty-one points in eighth grade, and to forty-six points in twelfth grade. Callahan (2013) reports that ELs are almost twice as likely to drop out as native and fluent English speakers. She adds that "the social and academic isolation of EL students educated in ESL programs perpetuates the notion of EL students' language deficiencies. The creation of separate, but not equal, EL contexts results in their social, academic and physical disengagement" (2). While ELs continue to underperform academically in the United States, their lack of proficiency in English is not the cause of their academic struggles. Instead the culprits tend to be the underfunded, overcrowded, unsafe schools they attend that have remedial-oriented curriculum, inadequate health and counseling services, and less experienced teachers and school leaders (Soltero and Soltero 2010). Carefully planned and well-implemented dual language programs can provide the type of enriched and culturally responsive education needed to narrow the achievement gap for ELs and other minority groups.

A Growing Interest in Dual Language Education

Language immersion education continues to receive worldwide attention by policy makers, educators, and the media. The proliferation of immersion programs in Europe, the Americas, and Asia is "due in large part to the strong research base that has consistently demonstrated the benefits of immersion education" (Tedick, Christian, and Fortune 2011, 5) and is increasingly viewed as an ideal model for all students to develop academic, biliterate, and cross-cultural competencies. As mentioned in the introduction, examples of this increased attention in the United States include the New York City Department of Education's recent expansion of its dual language programs, Utah's dual language immersion initiative, the statewide commitment in North Carolina to increasing dual language program offerings, Rhode Island as the first state in the country to approve statewide Dual Language Program Standards, and trends in teacher preparation programs that offer specialized university courses on dual language education.

As part of the New York City Department of Education's commitment to student achievement and to increasing multilingual programs across the city, in 2015 New York City School Chancellor Carmen Fariña launched an expansion of its dual language offerings by opening forty new programs. Fariña said, "In some ways we are all immigrant children, and as an English Learner, I know education makes the difference and these new dual language programs will give students new pathways to college or a meaningful career. We are also recognizing that speaking multiple languages is an asset for students, families, schools, and our entire City. As a part of these programs, our kids will learn new cultures, parents will come into classrooms in new ways, and together we will make this system the best urban school district in the country" (NYC DOE Press Release 2015). As of 2015, New York City reported to have 145 dual language programs in its public schools.

In 2008, the Utah Senate passed the International Initiative bill creating funding for dual language immersion programs in Spanish, Chinese, and French. Two years later, Governor Gary Herbert issued a challenge to Utah schools to open one hundred dual language programs. The Utah initiative articulates a "roadmap" for K–16 pathways: "The state's students will enter universities or the global workforce equipped with truly valuable language and cultural skills at the Advanced Level of proficiency in four skills areas" (Utah Language Roadmap for the 21st Century 2015). By 2015, Utah offered dual language programs in Spanish, Chinese, French, German, and Portuguese in 118 schools across twenty-two districts.

The North Carolina Board of Education recently committed to a number of initiatives that expand dual language programs. Part of a strategic plan to promote global education, the Board also committed to implementing at least one full dual language program that spans K–12 in each of the state's 115 districts, and partnering with colleges and universities to develop the special cadre of bilingual teachers and administrators. In Delaware, Governor Jack Markell emphasized the importance of learning world languages, stating that "Delaware graduates who enter the job market without the ability to speak a world language other than English are at a significant disadvantage." The Governor's World Language Expansion Initiative for K–16 includes dual language education, options for adding a third world language, Advanced Placement (AP) world language classes, and dual enrollment in college level language courses. In 2015, Rhode Island became the first state in the country to approve statewide Dual Language Program Standards. Rhode Island Education Commissioner Deborah Gist stated, "A large pool of people who are bilingual and biliterate has the potential to change the economic and social landscape of the state over time. One of the most effective investments that public school districts can make toward this end is to develop and maintain dual language programs for students in grades K–12." She added that the standards "assist districts in the design of the programs, planning for program implementation, maintenance of the programs once they are created, and improvements over time that will help ensure long-term success" (Memo to the Rhode Island Board of Education 2014).

The recognition that proficiency in more than one language is beneficial both for individuals and for society is supported by extensive research evidence that bilinguals experience cognitive and academic advantages, interact better with others, have more employment opportunities, and earn higher salaries (Callahan and Gándara 2014). Those who are biliterate have even more advantages, accessing more information and gaining more knowledge. They are also better able to interact with those from other linguistic and cultural backgrounds (de Jong 2011). By developing understandings of the languages, customs, and norms of other cultures, students in well-implemented dual language programs build stronger collaborations across diverse groups while becoming bilingual, biliterate, cross-cultural, and also achieving academically. Professional and academic bilingualism and biliteracy in turn increases cross-cultural knowledge, improves intergroup relations, and enhances economic competitiveness at home and abroad (Soltero 2011).

Seal of Biliteracy

Another compelling reason to offer dual language programs is the Seal of Biliteracy, which is being adopted across the United States. As mentioned in the introduction, twenty-one states plus the District of Columbia have passed legislation making the Seal of Biliteracy state law, and thirteen others are developing legislation. The Seal of Biliteracy is an official recognition awarded by a state's Department of Education to students who demonstrate biliterate competencies in a LOTE and English on a norm-referenced language exam in their senior year of high school. The Seal is included in students' diplomas and high school transcripts. In addition to awarding the Seal of Biliteracy upon graduation from high school, states and school districts also give biliteracy pathway awards in elementary and middle school that recognize and celebrate students' progress toward acquiring biliteracy in additive bilingual and world language programs. The national Seal of Biliteracy website (http:// sealofbiliteracy.org), outlines a number of goals in offering high school graduates opportunities to earn the Seal of Biliteracy:

- Encourage students to study languages.
- Certify students' biliteracy skills.
- Recognize the value of language diversity.
- Provide employers with a method of identifying people with biliteracy skills.
- Provide universities with a way to recognize and give credit to students who have high-level skills in multiple languages.
- Prepare students with twenty-first century skills that will benefit them in the labor market and global society.
- Strengthen intergroup relationships and honor the multiple cultures and languages in a community.

The four leading language education organizations—the National Association of Bilingual Education, the Teachers of English to Speakers of Other Languages International Association, the American Council on the Teaching of Foreign Languages, and the National Council of State Supervisors for Languages—drafted the recently released Guidelines for Implementing the Seal of Biliteracy (2015), which provide recommendations for implementation across the United States (http://sealofbiliteracy .org/state-guidelines). The Guidelines stipulate that proficiency should be demonstrated in social and academic use of both languages and suggest a number of ways that the LOTE can be assessed to determine adequate proficiency levels to earn the Seal of Biliteracy, such as AP or International Baccalaureate (IB) exams, Standards-Based Measurement of Proficiency, American Council on the Teaching of Foreign Languages Assessment of Performance Toward Proficiency in Languages, Tribal Language Assessments, Sign Language Proficiency Interview for American Sign Language, and other assessments aligned to the required minimum level for language proficiency.

A Cautionary Note About Dual Language Education

Initiatives for statewide and districtwide implementation of dual language programs such as the ones mentioned above are sometimes spearheaded either by foreign language teachers and/or by middle-class families, mostly White non-Latinos, who want their children to be bilingual. This may result in two-way dual language programs that are made up of mostly White, non-Latino, middle-class, native English-speaking students, and mostly lower-income minority ELs. Without careful planning, this can have potentially damaging consequences for ELs. A study conducted by Cortina, Makar, and Mount-Cors (2015) suggested that "some parent-driven programs were supported by parents who were better educated, better informed, and wealthier than other parents, which resulted in elitist programs" (11). The authors add that schools need "to address the power imbalance . . . so that such programs do not become merely foreign language programs for the more affluent students" (11). When these power-differentials are minimized, two-way dual language programs can serve as a bridge for authentic integration between families and students from different social classes and cultural backgrounds. Palmer and Martínez (2013) add that teachers must engage in professional development "that reflects both current theoretical understandings of language practices in bilingual communities and a more critically contextualized understanding of the power dynamics that operate in bilingual classroom contexts" (269).

Almost twenty years ago, Guadalupe Valdés brought to light these very risks that still resonate as race- and class-based struggles continue in the United States. Valdés (1997) raised concerns that the needs and desires of the dominant group and the dominant language (English) can take precedent over the academic and linguistic needs of ELs. For example, in the early grades, native English speakers require more repetition and modified LOTE so they can understand and develop content in their L2. Meanwhile, LOTE-speaking children need higher levels of academic L1 since they already have conversational language. Gándara and Callahan (2014) add, "Dual language programs provide a viable model for the integration of students from different social and linguistic backgrounds while also providing the advantage of a rigorous curriculum in two languages. However, the caveat remains that without careful attention paid to students' social integration and the development of hierarchies, dual language education can easily prioritize the foreign language learning of native English speakers over the academic development of minority youth" (292).

Valdés contends that English-speaking students tend to dominate classroom talk as well as teachers' time, diverting attention from Spanish-dominant students. This mirrors what happens in parent meetings, during which White non-Latino parents commonly outspeak non-English-speaking parents. The intergroup relations between these two very different groups are another area of concern, which must be carefully thought out so that students and families from both groups interact in and outside of the classroom in positive ways (Carey et al. 2010). While there is a call for less linguistic isolation and more integration of ELs with their English-speaking peers, there may be a perceived or real case that ELs' L1 is exploited in two-way dual language programs for the benefit of native English-speaking students. An effective two-way program must address the racial, ethnic, and income diversity of its students in thoughtful and concrete ways, illustrated by the experiences at Rocha Public School District, an affluent suburban district with three Spanish-English dual language schools.

Students in this high-performing school district came mostly from two ethnic and income family backgrounds: White non-Latino middle class and Latino working class. Little attention was given to the relationship between these two groups in the first few years of implementation. The only interaction was inside the classroom walls and only among students. There was little interaction outside the classroom or among families. All parent meetings were separated by language, and there were few opportunities for families to intermingle. In the community, the relationship between these groups was mainly one of employee or provider of services (Latinos), and employer or customer (White non-Latinos). Mrs. Cruz and Mrs. Wynn, who served on the district dual language parent committee, noticed that students from the two language groups at their respective schools often separated themselves in the cafeteria and the playground. As they began to talk to other parents, they realized that this type of separation was also happening among families in their schools. They contacted the district family liaison and began to talk about ways for the district to create opportunities for families to interact during and after school hours.

The first adjustment was in parent meetings, which now began with parents from both language groups together for general announcements and recognitions, and then had breakout sessions by language for the remainder of the meetings. Originally they had the entire time together, but the translations made meetings too long and tedious. Mrs. Cruz and Mrs. Wynn, together with the dual language parent committee, also encouraged family members who were either bilingual or had some proficiency in the L2 to attend each other's language breakout sessions. Pretty soon, some White non-Latino parents were attending the Spanish breakout sessions and some Latino Spanish-dominant parents were attending the English sessions. This created meaningful opportunities not just to interact with each other, but also to use their L2. With the help of the district family liaison, the three schools created a number of very successful events, projects, and programs where families interacted socially, including dual language family nights, cross-cultural and international fairs, multicultural talent shows, and language clubs. The most popular after-school activities were the parent cooking club and salsa dancing after-school classes.

Families from both language groups also began to initiate and participate in advocacy efforts, such as requesting that district information like websites, school newsletters, and report cards be provided in both languages. The joint advocacy efforts had positive results. After reallocating funds, the district hired two Latino bilingual parents who were former teachers in Mexico to translate district and school information, including a comprehensive bilingual dual language link on the district website. In another instance, when the Rocha Superintendent and School Board

[handwritten margin note: model to integrate different parents of Eng/span language together]

decided not to expand dual language to middle school, parents from both language groups came together to organize a petition in favor of continuing the program, not just to middle school but also into high school. They collected enough signatures from the community that the Board changed its decision and began expansion plans for the program. This type of collaboration not only values and uses the linguistic and cultural capital of families, but also helps to form strong relationships and build understanding between families.

Rationale for Implementing a Dual Language Program

Bilingual education models for ELs fall under two categories: (1) additive programs—such as maintenance, developmental, heritage language, and dual language—that promote biliteracy and include bilingual instruction for an extended period of time, and (2) subtractive programs—transitional bilingual education—that use the L1 only until ELs become proficient in English.

What sets two-way dual language apart from all other language programs is the opportunity to develop biliteracy and cross-cultural competencies alongside speakers of both LOTE and English. Because the languages and cultures represented in the school and community are seen as assets, everyone comes to the table with valuable contributions. This type of additive education embraces diversity and creates linguistic and cultural bridges between diverse groups. Two-way programs offer the best environment for native speakers of LOTE and English to serve as language models for each other through extended opportunities to interact academically and socially. For teachers and staff, dual language presents ongoing opportunities to collaborate with, learn from, and support each other. Because general education teachers increasingly have ELs in their classrooms, they often find themselves unsure about how to address their academic and linguistic needs. By participating in dual language programs, they can acquire knowledge about second language acquisition, L2 instructional practices, and cross-cultural understandings from their bilingual teacher partners. The resulting collaborations between bilingual and general program teachers afford a much-needed bridge between the traditionally segregated bilingual/ESL teachers and programs, and the rest of the school community (Soltero 2004).

Research on the Effectiveness of Dual Language Education

Collier and Thomas (2014) emphasize the need to acknowledge the extensive research of the many benefits that come from achieving biliterate and multilingual proficiencies. These benefits extend beyond students to make positive changes for families, communities, and society, "transforming the way that human beings relate to teach other across all their differences" (xv). The effectiveness of dual language education has been well documented both within and outside the United States, especially in Canada and Europe.

In their original longitudinal study, Collier and Thomas (2004) found that ELs who participated in dual language education outperformed comparable monolingual-schooled students in academic achievement after four to seven years in the program. Students who received dual language instruction for at least five to six years reached the fiftieth percentile on the reading standardized tests in English by fifth or sixth grade and maintained this level of performance in subsequent grades. The results also indicated that native English speakers maintained their English, acquired the L2, and achieved well above the fiftieth percentile in all content areas on norm-referenced tests in English. They found that by sixth grade, ELs in dual language were ahead in English achievement compared to students in early-exit transitional bilingual or ESL pullout programs. Achievement in English standardized tests for ELs was close to those of native English speakers (around the fiftieth percentile). By eleventh grade, ELs in dual language programs scored above the average level for native English speakers on standardized tests in English compared to ELs in the other programs. Thomas and Collier conclude that for students to achieve grade-level competencies, they must receive at least four years of schooling in the L1 and at least four years of schooling in the L2.

A more recent analysis conducted in North Carolina by Thomas and Collier (2012) examined the reading and math test scores of students enrolled in two-way Spanish-English dual language programs in grades 3–8 from 2007 to 2010 in seven districts. The findings showed that students scored significantly higher in reading in fourth grade than their peers who were not in dual language programs. They found this trend continued through eighth grade. By fifth grade, dual language students scored the same as their monolingual peers a grade ahead of them. In the math test scores, fifth-grade dual language students scored as high as their sixth-grade peers and continued their gains through eighth grade. The study found that dual language programs were particularly successful in raising scores for African American, special education, and low-income students, as well as ELs. African American students scored at least one grade higher in reading than their peers not in dual language as early as fourth grade. In math, African American students were more than two grades ahead of African American nondual language students as early as fifth grade. Special education students in two-way programs outscored their peers who were not in dual language. Thomas and Collier suggest that the benefits for special education students are likely due to the cognitive stimulation that results from engaging with the curriculum in two languages and by acquiring the L2. They concluded that "two-way dual language classes increase the reading and math achievement of all students regardless of subgroup, and are a substantially effective means of addressing North Carolina's large achievement gaps for limited-English-proficient students, non-language-minority native-English-speaking African American students, students of low-socioeconomic status, and special education students" (83).

In another influential longitudinal and cross-sectional study, Lindholm-Leary (2001) found that native English speakers developed high levels of proficiency in their L1 regardless of whether they participated in total (90-10) or partial (50-50) dual language programs. In addition, students from both language groups developed high levels of L2 proficiency in both total and partial immersion models, though their proficiency was higher in total immersion programs. The results show that both total and partial dual language models promote proficiency in two languages, although students developed higher levels of bilingualism in total immersion models. Native English speakers did not vary in their L1 proficiency according to their participation in total or partial programs. English-speaking students who received as little as ten or twenty percent of their instruction in English scored as well as English-dominant students who received their instruction in English fifty percent of the time. These findings were true for African American, Latino, and White non-Latino students, and did not vary according to their socioeconomic status. Spanish speakers benefited more than English speakers from total immersion than from partial immersion, supporting the critical role of ELs' L1 development in developing English (Genesee et al. 2006). English speakers in total immersion scored higher in Spanish proficiency than those in partial immersion programs. For Spanish-speaking students, the program model was not a factor in English development. Spanish-speaking students who received considerably less English instruction in total immersion than Spanish speakers who received fifty percent of instruction in English in partial immersion scored about the same in English tests. Receiving less English instruction in 90-10 programs did not negatively affect Spanish speakers.

In literacy and academic attainment, Lindholm-Leary found that English- and Spanish-speaking students made significant growth in reading and academic achievement in both the L1 and L2 across grade levels, and scored on par with their peers using standardized norms for English and Spanish speakers. The results showed that higher levels of bilingual proficiency were associated with better reading achievement, corresponding with other research findings that point to higher levels of bilingual proficiency leading to increased academic and cognitive functioning (Goldenberg and Coleman 2010). Spanish- and English-dominant students in dual language programs outperformed their peers across California in English reading and academic achievement tests. With regard to content, Lindholm-Leary's study showed that students in dual language functioned at grade level or above in two languages in the content areas and scored on par with their peers across California.

The research in the last decade demonstrates positive effects and gains for students who participate in dual language education. Lindholm-Leary (2012) summarizes additional key findings from more recent studies conducted in elementary, middle, and high schools (Garcia 2009; Howard and Sugarman 2007; Lindholm-Leary 2008,

2012, 2014; Lindholm-Leary and Hernandez 2011; Lindholm-Leary and Borsato 2005, 2006). The findings concur that students in dual language programs:

- perform at or above grade level on standardized reading and math tests in English
- score similar to their statewide peers by about fifth to seventh grade, if not sooner
- achieve at or above grade level in reading (and math) tests measured in the L2
- close the achievement gap compared to English-only classrooms by about fifth grade.

Compared to students in general education programs, students in middle and high school dual language programs are:

- as or more likely to be enrolled in higher-level math courses
- as or more likely to pass high school exit exams
- less likely to drop out of school
- more likely to close the achievement gap by the end of high school.

Even though most of the research has focused on Spanish-English programs, the results also extend to studies of Chinese and Korean dual language programs. These and other research studies on additive bilingual education provide a critical platform for the development and understanding of dual language programs, that when well planned and implemented, produce high academic outcomes for all students. These research findings offer the necessary empirical evidence to guide program implementation and to contest misguided perspectives and practices about bilingual education.

Non-Negotiables: Dual Language Program Criteria

The Center for Applied Linguistics Directory of Two-Way Immersion Programs in the U.S. currently lists 458 dual language programs, a significant increase from 1990 when there were fewer than forty programs listed. The majority of the programs are implemented in grades PK–6, with approximately one-fifth in middle or high schools. Of the programs listed in the directory, the majority are Spanish-English, with a few French-English, Chinese-English, Korean-English, Japanese-English, German-English, and Navajo-English. Because the directory is self-reported, the number of dual language programs in the United States is likely much higher. Due to the tremendous increase in dual language programs in recent years and the variations of model implementation, the Directory limits the inclusion of programs only to those that meet the criteria listed below (see Figure 1-6 and Figure 1-7).

Researchers agree that acquiring academic L2 generally takes five to seven years in comparison to conversational L1, which may take anywhere from six months to

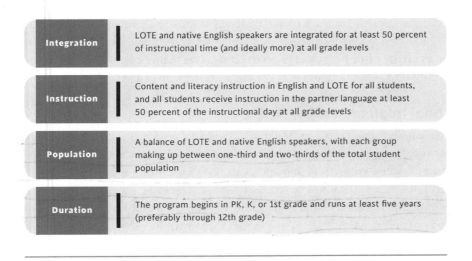

FIGURE **1-6**
Elementary (K–5) Two-Way Dual Language Programs Criteria

Integration	LOTE and native English speakers are integrated for at least 50 percent of instructional time (and ideally more) at all grade levels
Instruction	Content and literacy instruction in English and LOTE for all students, and all students receive instruction in the partner language at least 50 percent of the instructional day at all grade levels
Population	A balance of LOTE and native English speakers, with each group making up between one-third and two-thirds of the total student population
Duration	The program begins in PK, K, or 1st grade and runs at least five years (preferably through 12th grade)

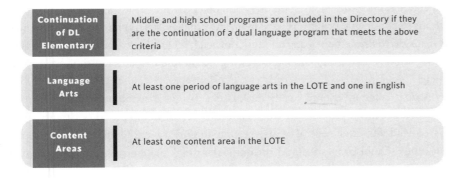

FIGURE **1-7**
Middle and High School Dual Language Programs Criteria

Continuation of DL Elementary	Middle and high school programs are included in the Directory if they are the continuation of a dual language program that meets the above criteria
Language Arts	At least one period of language arts in the LOTE and one in English
Content Areas	At least one content area in the LOTE

two years (Cummins 2001). For students to develop high levels of biliteracy and cross-cultural competencies, they should participate in the program a minimum of six to eight years. Therefore, designing dual language programs that continue into middle and high school significantly enhances students' academic and literacy proficiencies in the L2 and better prepares them to continue into advanced language classes in college and beyond.

Variations in Dual Language Models

While dual language program models include a wide variety of organizational structures, all share three common goals: biliterate, academic, and cross-cultural competencies. These three universal goals guide all decision making in how programs are structured. Program models may include differences in scope of implementation (strand or schoolwide), student language population served (one-way with ELs only or two-way with ELs and native English speakers), language allocation (total or partial immersion), language of initial literacy instruction (sequential or simultaneous), and classroom organization (self-contained or team-teaching). The following section briefly explains each of these structures (see Figure 1-8). Factors to consider when deciding what options to choose will be further discussed in Chapter 2.

School Implementation Scope

Dual language programs can be implemented schoolwide or as a strand. Schoolwide programs tend to have better results for a number of reasons. The entire school shares the same vision, mission, and goals. Everyone, from office staff to physical education teachers, commits to a collective vision, creating a sense of unity, understanding, and common direction that reduces competition for resources among other school programs. de Jong (2011) argues that when the program is implemented schoolwide, "it is easier to establish bilingualism as the norm for the school" (211). In addition, the tracking and segregation inherent in a strand is absent in schoolwide models, and student attrition does not affect them as much as strand programs. Although schoolwide programs have many advantages, several factors may influence the decision to implement a strand model instead, including the number of bilingual teachers in the school, flexibility in testing accountability in English, and district policies.

A dual language strand can be just as effective as a schoolwide program, provided that potential problems are considered, such as mobility and declining numbers of students after several years, incompatibility or competition for resources with other school programs, and misunderstandings or opposition from non-dual language participants, including students, teachers, and families. Student mobility is particularly challenging in dual language strands because there is typically only one classroom per grade level, so an initial class that starts with twenty-five children in kindergarten may end up with only ten or fifteen students by the time the

FIGURE **1-8**
What's What in Dual Language: Getting the Terminology Right

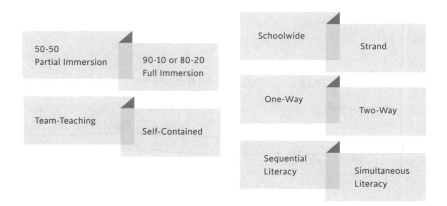

program reaches fourth or fifth grade. Accepting new monolingual English-speaking students after second grade is not recommended, because the curriculum becomes more demanding and less contextualized in third grade and beyond. Monolingual English-speaking students who enter the program after second grade have great difficulty understanding academic concepts in the LOTE.

Language Allocation

Total and partial immersion are the two program models in dual language education. Partial immersion, also known as 50-50 or balanced model, provides instruction in both languages in equal amounts of time at all grade levels—the LOTE fifty percent of the time and English the other fifty percent of the time. Content areas are commonly taught in both languages by alternating between each language by time or teacher. In 50-50 models that use team-teaching, students alternate days between the English and the LOTE teacher to receive content instruction in both languages. In self-contained classrooms, the bilingual teacher alternates instruction in each language by day or week in the early grades. In middle and high school, the languages are distributed by content and/or teacher. For the most part, all high school dual language programs are partial immersion where the language allocation is distributed among content periods.

Total immersion is almost always in elementary programs and includes two models: 90-10 and 80-20. The initial amount of instruction in the LOTE and English corresponds to the amount of time indicated by the ratio: in the LOTE ninety percent or eighty percent of the time and in English ten percent or twenty percent of the time, usually from PK–first to second grade. In second or third grade, instruction in English increases to twenty percent or thirty percent, while instruction in the LOTE decreases to eighty percent or seventy percent. By the time students reach fourth or fifth grade, there is a balance of instructional time in both languages. It is worth mentioning that the program does not become a 50-50 model, just the language allocation. While the language allocation becomes half and half in fourth or fifth grade and above, the program continues to be an 80-20 or 90-10 model (see Figure 1-9). Total immersion immerses students in the LOTE in the initial years of the program, but includes English instruction for a small portion of the day. All academic content areas are initially taught in the LOTE with a gradual shift to instruction of content areas in both languages by fourth or fifth grade. For example, in second grade, math may be partially taught in English, while science and social studies continue to be in the LOTE. The next year, both math and social studies may be taught in English and science continues to be taught in the LOTE. By fourth or fifth grade, all content areas are either taught in both languages, alternating by day, week, or month, or each content area is assigned a language of instruction (for example, math in English and science in the LOTE).

FIGURE **1-9**
Dual Language Program
Models Spanish-English

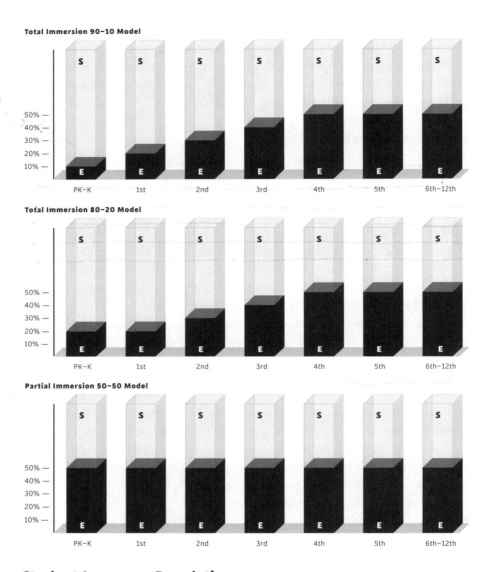

Student Language Population

Dual language programs are either implemented as one-way or two-way models (see Figure 1-10) or sometimes a combination of both within a school. One-way programs can either have just dominant-language students with no speakers of the target language (such as English immersion programs for Korean speakers in Korea or

FIGURE **1-10**
Dual Language Models
Based on Students' First
Language

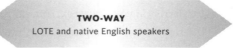

French immersion programs for English speakers in Canada), or all students are not yet proficient in the language of schooling. In the United States, ELs are the most common student population in one-way programs where they learn English as a second language while developing academic language in their L1. Once students reach proficiency in English, they are not exited from the program but continue to develop academic LOTE and English. This model is sometimes known as late-exit developmental or maintenance bilingual education. In the two-way model, students are from two language groups—typically ELs that speak the same L1 and native English speakers—ideally with fifty percent of the students from each language. Students who are bilingual or heritage language speakers often also participate in this type of dual language model. Heritage language speakers include bilingual students who are more proficient in English or those who come from the LOTE culture but are no longer proficient in their heritage language. They might therefore be considered native English speakers depending on the level of language loss they have experienced.

Classroom Configurations

Dual language programs implement either self-contained (sometimes called roller-coaster) or team-teaching (sometimes called side-by-side), or a combination of both (see Figure 1-11). The decision to have team-teaching or self-contained classrooms depends on the language proficiencies of the existing teachers in the school, access to bilingual teachers, and/or teacher interest. In strand programs that have two classrooms per grade level, those teachers can either team-teach or be self-contained.

In self-contained classrooms, one bilingual teacher conducts all instruction in both languages, which can be separated by time, day, or content. The classroom has instructional materials and print in both languages. In 50-50 models, books, posters, bulletins, and other classroom print are equally represented in each language. In 90-10 or 80-20 models, there should be more print and other instructional materials in the LOTE in the early grades, eventually reaching an equal amount by fourth or fifth grade. Self-contained teachers in two-way models can group students in heterogeneous (LOTE and native English speakers together) and homogenous language

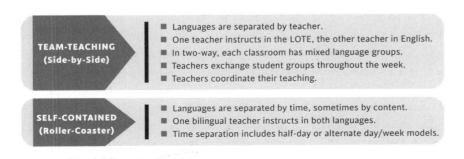

TEAM-TEACHING (Side-by-Side)
- Languages are separated by teacher.
- One teacher instructs in the LOTE, the other teacher in English.
- In two-way, each classroom has mixed language groups.
- Teachers exchange student groups throughout the week.
- Teachers coordinate their teaching.

SELF-CONTAINED (Roller-Coaster)
- Languages are separated by time, sometimes by content.
- One bilingual teacher instructs in both languages.
- Time separation includes half-day or alternate day/week models.

FIGURE **1-11**
Classroom Configurations: Team-Teaching and Self-Contained

groups. LOTE and native English speakers can be separated for certain instruction like ESL or LOTE as a second language (LOTE-SL). For content area instruction in a two-way model, students from both languages are combined in cooperative learning groups and the teacher alternates between each language by time, day, or content. Scheduling in self-contained classrooms requires teachers to be very organized and have excellent time-management skills. The teacher may alternate between the LOTE and English every other day, every other week, or even every other month or quarter, depending on the grade level. For middle and high school programs, designated bilingual content teachers typically instruct entirely in the LOTE because students take other classes only in English.

In team-teaching, two teachers instruct in two separate classrooms or together within one classroom. In elementary programs, both teachers can be bilingual, each responsible for one language, or one teacher is bilingual and the other monolingual in English. In most schools, each teacher has her/his own classroom and each is responsible for both groups of students. The class rosters of each teacher have students from both language groups. It is not a good idea for students to be assigned to the class roster of the teacher that speaks their dominant language because students should not be segregated by language according to the language of the teacher, but rather be integrated with native speakers and the L2 teacher. For example, it is not a good idea to have only Chinese-speaking ELs on the class roster of the bilingual Chinese teacher and only native English-speaking students on the class roster of the monolingual English teacher. For middle and high school, team-teaching can be organized between content area bilingual teachers or between monolingual English and bilingual content teachers.

Instructional materials, such as books, classroom print, displays, and technology are all in the language assigned to that teacher and classroom. For example, in an Arabic-English team-teaching dual language program, the majority of the instructional materials are in Arabic in the Arabic teacher's classroom, while the majority of the instructional materials in the English teacher's classroom are in English. Students travel between the two classrooms for instruction and are grouped in integrated mixed-group clusters for instruction and social interaction for most of the day. In the early grades especially, students may also be grouped by language either for L1 literacy development or L2 instruction. The mixed-language student groups alternate between the two teachers for content, literacy, and L2 instruction. Since the two languages are naturally kept separate by room and teacher, students generally alternate languages between the two rooms by time of day (morning and afternoon) or by day. In addition to good time management and organization, team-teaching also requires collaborative teamwork and well-coordinated ongoing planning.

Decisions on whether to do self-contained or team-teaching depends on school circumstances and teacher preference. Weilan's first year of teaching was in a two-way 50-50 Chinese dual language program, so she felt lucky to have been assigned a partner who had taught in the program for several years. Her partner was very open-minded and committed to dual language education. They complemented each other because they shared similar views and approaches to teaching and learning and were open to each other's ideas. Later, due to changes in staff and student enrollment, Weilan taught as a self-contained teacher for several years. Although she enjoyed having her own classroom with the flexibility to go at her own pace and not being accountable to a partner, she felt that teaching the curriculum in two languages and preparing two language arts lessons each day with thirty-two students was very challenging. In Weilan's twelve years of teaching in dual language programs, she taught both as a team-teacher and a self-contained teacher. In reflecting on which of these two options she preferred to teach, for Weilan the answer depends on whether one likes to teach collaboratively or alone, and whether the two partners get along at a personal level and see eye-to-eye at a pedagogical level. For Weilan, collaborating with another teacher was very rewarding not just because she could bounce ideas off of her partner, but also because the workload and responsibilities were shared. On the other hand, Weilan thinks that with the right conditions (small class size), self-contained teaching can also be very gratifying because there is more flexibility and the teacher is only responsible for one classroom and can adjust the pace to the students more easily.

Weilan's

PreK – second grade

Language of Emergent Literacy

In the early grades, typically PK through second, emergent literacy instruction can be sequential or simultaneous (see Figure 1-12). In sequential literacy instruction, students learn to read and write in their L1 first. After they have acquired the foundations of literacy in the L1, they transfer those skills to the L2 and learn specific literacy elements that pertain to the L2. For example, in a Spanish-English

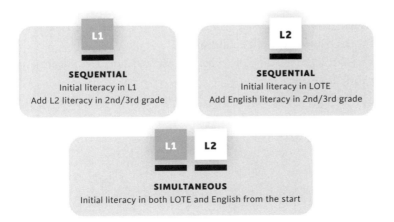

L1

SEQUENTIAL
Initial literacy in L1
Add L2 literacy in 2nd/3rd grade

L2

SEQUENTIAL
Initial literacy in LOTE
Add English literacy in 2nd/3rd grade

L1 **L2**

SIMULTANEOUS
Initial literacy in both LOTE and English from the start

FIGURE **1-12**
Two Approaches to Initial Literacy Instruction in Grades PK–1

two-way dual language program, Spanish-dominant students learn *sílabas* and English-dominant students learn phonics up until about second grade. Sequential literacy can also happen in two-way programs where all students learn how to read and write first in the LOTE. That is, both ELs and native English-speaking students learn to read and write in the non-English language first. This is more common in 90-10 models where all students are immersed in the LOTE in the early grades. In simultaneous literacy instruction, students learn to read and write in both languages at the same time. Part of the literacy block is conducted in English and part in the LOTE.

In most 50-50 two-way programs, emergent literacy instruction is typically in the students' L1. Conducting initial literacy instruction in the L2 in the early grades for native English speakers in a 50-50 two-way program is challenging for two reasons. First, English-dominant students do not have sufficient exposure to the LOTE and so have not developed a strong enough language base in kindergarten to begin LOTE literacy instruction in first grade. Second, English-dominant students usually do not have LOTE exposure at home to support literacy development in their L2. For ELs, the same challenges apply.

Decisions on whether to implement sequential or simultaneous literacy instruction, strand or schoolwide program, one-way or two-way model, total or partial immersion, and self-contained or team-teaching, all need to be made according to the particular characteristics and needs of each school. These decisions must take into account the vision and goals of families and the school, district or state restrictions or policies, the language/s of students in the school, the existing school staff's language skills, access to qualified bilingual teachers and support staff, and availability of high-quality instructional materials in the LOTE.

Suggestions for Further Reading

Callahan, Rebecca M., and Patricia C. Gándara. 2014. *The Bilingual Advantage: Language, Literacy and the US Labor Market*. Buffalo, NY: Multilingual Matters.

García, Ofelia. 2009. *Bilingual Education in the 21st Century: A Global Perspective*. New York: Wiley-Blackwell Publishing.

Shin, Sarah J. 2013. *Bilingualism in School and Society: Language, Identity, and Policy*. New York: Routledge. ✳

Dual Language Program Planning

Educators developing new programs or reviewing the effectiveness of existing programs can rest assured that over forty-five years of scientific evidence confirms that school-age children are able to mature and thrive in these programs. A great deal of effort goes into creating a quality dual language program. However, there is tremendous satisfaction in knowing that dual language students have what it take to be successful in the globalized communities in which they will be living. It is education for the future.

—Else Hamayan, Fred Genesee, and Nancy Cloud,
Dual Language Instruction from A to Z

[handwritten notes: Group two → Amada 25 – 29 pages. 11:45]

[handwritten: Amada]

Effective and sustainable dual language programs share one critical element: at least one full year of planning before implementation. Planning ensures that programs begin with the strongest possible footing and with all the necessary elements to create long-lasting and well-functioning models. Even before initial information is gathered and the planning phase is conceptualized, school leaders, teachers, and families must consider the many issues that could affect the implementation of the program. These factors may include student mobility rates, levels of family involvement, extent of teacher and family buy-in, languages spoken by students and their families, teacher qualifications and knowledge, and access to professional development. The long-term success or failure of a program partly depends on the decisions made prior to its implementation. Lindholm-Leary (2012) points out that "there are also important challenges in DLE [dual language education] that can impact the quality of these programs; that is, how well the programs are designed and implemented. These concerns include issues related to program design, accountability, curriculum and instruction as related to biliteracy, and bilingual language development" (258). Understanding each of the components of a well-designed program and how these fit together creates the foundation for informed decision making (see Figure 2-1). In dual language education, theory guides practice while research provides the necessary empirical evidence. Ongoing professional development enhances

be a DOE Employee ... open market account for me?

FIGURE **2-1**
Dual Language
Fundamentals

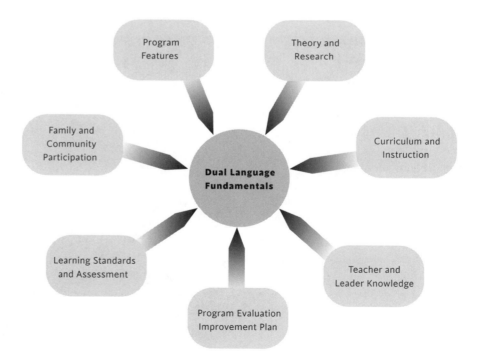

teacher and school leader knowledge of dual language, while family and community participation support program quality and sustainability.

The Planning Year: What to Expect

The year of planning is an intense process that needs to start early and be carefully thought out. Schools adopt new curricular practices in response to what appear to be constant changes in instructional programs, methods, assessments, and standards. Teachers and school leaders feel increasingly overwhelmed trying to keep up with national, state, and district policy shifts and demands. Therefore, the decision-making process must be responsive to school needs and inclusive of all stakeholders. School leaders should seek consensus to implement a dual language program by creating many opportunities for discussion, reflection, and shared decision making. Top-down directives from district administrators or school leaders typically result in weak or short-lived programs. A more effective approach is to build school buy-in *before* the program is implemented. Because dual language requires a substantial amount of work and ongoing attention on the part of teachers and school leaders, a well-planned program can cut down on the types of problems that typically arise in the first few years. Investing at least one entire year for planning pays off in the long run, as the experiences and success of the program at the Fusang Elementary Academy show.

After much discussion and deliberation, families, teachers, and school leaders at Fusang Elementary decided to implement a schoolwide two-way Mandarin-English dual language program, starting with PK–K. During several early meetings, the discussion focused on the needed balanced number of students from each language, family support, and bilingual qualifications of teachers and staff. The next step was to determine whether to implement a total or partial immersion model. Many parents and teachers expressed concerns about implementing an 80-20 model because they feared students would fall behind academically and not develop strong literacy skills in English. Some teachers also had reservations about the effects of student mobility on program effectiveness. Although teachers and parents had visited two nearby schools implementing 50-50 models, they had not observed any 80-20 programs. Two teachers who attended a national dual language conference brought back information and research about both models. Based on all the information gathered, they concluded that the school had the right "ingredients" to implement an 80-20 model since they had near-balanced student representation of the two languages and many teachers had bilingual endorsements. Because the school had been implementing bilingual and Mandarin foreign language programs for some time, they had a significant amount of Chinese instructional materials. In addition, parents were very supportive of their children continuing to build their Chinese language and heritage pride.

Those teachers who supported the total immersion model shared information about the pros and cons for each model, invited a dual language expert to talk to families and staff, and arranged for a daylong visit to a school implementing an 80-20 model in a nearby city. All this proved to be successful in convincing families, teachers, and the principal that the school could effectively implement a total immersion model. The teachers and principal also made a yearlong plan for professional development and family workshops to increase their understanding of second language acquisition and dual language education. After ten years of implementation and several changes in district and school administrators, the full immersion dual language program at Fusang Elementary Academy continues to thrive, so much so that the school has a waiting list because so many parents want their children in the program.

Differences Across Elementary, Middle, and High School

While the fundamental premises of dual language education (goals, professional development, etc.) apply across the different grade spans, some components differ between elementary, middle, and high school (see Figure 2-2). Elementary schools, typically grades PK–6, are sometimes configured as PK–2 or PK–5. The language allocation in the elementary grades where one teacher teaches all content areas is usually by time, and sometimes by content or by teacher (in team-teaching contexts).

FIGURE **2-2**
Differences Between Elementary School and Middle and High School Programs

	ELEMENTARY SCHOOL (PK–6)	MIDDLE AND HIGH SCHOOL (7–12)
Classrooms	• Self-contained	• Departmentalized
Curriculum	• Core content and specials (preps)	• Core content and electives • Service learning
Language Allocation	• 90-10, 80-20, or 50-50 • Time-based	• 50-50 • Period-based • Dependent on master schedule
Teachers	• One or two teachers • Multidisciplinary • Grade-level teams	• Multiple teachers • Content specialists • Department heads
Guidance	• Classroom teacher • Parents	• Counselors • College and career paths
Size	• Fewer students/teachers • Smaller teacher-student ratio	• More numbers of students/teachers • Larger teacher-student ratio
Extracurricular	• Assemblies • After school	• Student government • Event planning and clubs

In middle school (generally grades 7–8) and high school (grades 9–12), core subjects are departmentalized and taught by different teachers specializing in each content area. For these grades, the language allocation is based on content area teachers with separate content periods. Scheduling is one of the most challenging parts of dual language regardless of the grade band, but it is especially so in middle and high school programs.

In addition to differences in how content areas are taught, high schools tend to have many more students and programs, larger class sizes, less family involvement, electives that compete for students' interests, and more extracurricular activities. Student government, student associations, and clubs are a big part of high school culture in the United States, but are typically not as much in elementary school. In high schools, various student groups plan events like homecoming, prom, and graduation while others are involved in committees like yearbook, school newspaper, and radio show. Student clubs often include areas that are relevant to dual language education like culture and language clubs, advocacy and social justice clubs, and international clubs. In contrast to elementary schools, high schools have social workers and counselors who address students' developmental needs and provide career/college pathway advice. In addition, many high schools also have a service-learning component that requires students to do volunteer work in the community.

Dual language education in high school should not be thought of as a stand-alone curriculum (like science or fine arts), but rather be viewed as a comprehensive program that incorporates all aspects of high school dual language students' experiences. For example, the service-learning component could be coordinated with relevant language and cultural experiences, like volunteering in a nearby elementary dual language program or a center for the elderly where the LOTE is spoken. Other types of coordination with the dual language program can include incorporating the LOTE and its cultures in major school events, like homecoming and graduation. Extracurricular programs and clubs can reflect relevant cross-cultural and biliterate activities that support and promote dual language goals.

Many elementary dual language programs have no pathways to high school dual language, so program expansion plans should be thought out early on, especially in districts that have significant numbers of elementary programs. Articulation between elementary, middle, and high school is critical in providing pathways for bilingual students to continue their biliteracy development through the secondary grades and into college. Figure 2-3 provides a snapshot of what a PK–16 articulation and vertical alignment can look like. The long-term plan discussed later in this chapter further explains this vertical articulation and program expansion.

FIGURE **2-3**
Dual Language Pathways
PK–16

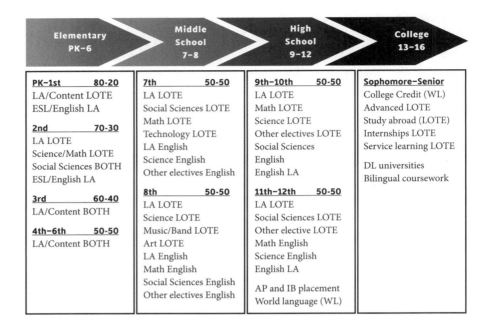

Elementary PK–6	Middle School 7–8	High School 9–12	College 13–16
PK–1st 80-20 LA/Content LOTE ESL/English LA **2nd 70-30** LA LOTE Science/Math LOTE Social Sciences BOTH ESL/English LA **3rd 60-40** LA/Content BOTH **4th–6th 50-50** LA/Content BOTH	**7th 50-50** LA LOTE Social Sciences LOTE Math LOTE Technology LOTE LA English Science English Other electives English **8th 50-50** LA LOTE Science LOTE Music/Band LOTE Art LOTE LA English Math English Social Sciences English Other electives English	**9th–10th 50-50** LA LOTE Math LOTE Science LOTE Other electives LOTE Social Sciences English English LA **11th–12th 50-50** LA LOTE Social Sciences LOTE Other elective LOTE Math English Science English English LA AP and IB placement World language (WL)	**Sophomore–Senior** College Credit (WL) Advanced LOTE Study abroad (LOTE) Internships LOTE Service learning LOTE DL universities Bilingual coursework

Planning a Dual Language Program

Strategic planning is a systematic and comprehensive process focused on the long-term success of a program, and involves gathering information, including families and communities, conducting school visits, participating in professional development, and creating a plan of action (see Figure 2-4). A good starting point then is to gather and analyze information on dual language as well as other forms of bilingual or world language immersion programs.

Many sources of information on dual language education are available in print and online, including books, articles, professional organizations, and blogs (see Appendix B for a list of videos, professional organizations, and information/research centers). Research studies, like those outlined in Chapter 1, provide empirical evidence of program effectiveness. One very comprehensive resource is Dual Language Education of New Mexico (www.dlenm.org), a nonprofit organization that provides information on the development and implementation of dual language education. The site offers a wide variety of resources, including the Soleado newsletter, e-bulletins, information on program development, samples of curriculum and schedules, conferences and professional development, promotion and advocacy, instruction and assessment, as well as family and community involvement. Dual Language Education of New Mexico also offers a paid subscription that provides access to additional resources, videos, and networking. Another organization is the National Dual Language Consortium (www.dual-language.org), which aims to "coordinate,

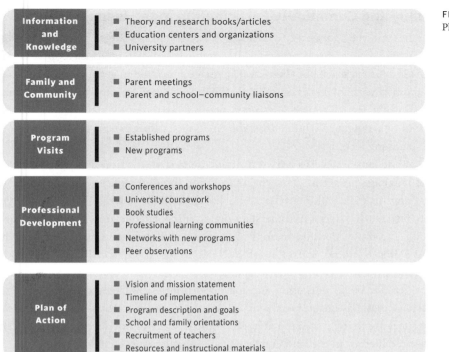

FIGURE **2-4**
Planning Steps

Information and Knowledge
- Theory and research books/articles
- Education centers and organizations
- University partners

Family and Community
- Parent meetings
- Parent and school–community liaisons

Program Visits
- Established programs
- New programs

Professional Development
- Conferences and workshops
- University coursework
- Book studies
- Professional learning communities
- Networks with new programs
- Peer observations

Plan of Action
- Vision and mission statement
- Timeline of implementation
- Program description and goals
- School and family orientations
- Recruitment of teachers
- Resources and instructional materials

consolidate and disseminate resources and research and make them available to support dual language education." Members of this consortium include the Center for Applied Linguistics, the Illinois Resource Center, Two-Way and Dual Language Education, the Center for Advanced Research on Language Acquisition, and Dual Language Education of New Mexico.

Partnering with colleges and universities provides added sources of information and research data that support the implementation and sustainability of dual language programs. Faculty and graduate students who conduct research on dual language education and related fields can be tapped to support planning and implementation efforts. Partnerships with research centers facilitate the documentation of program effectiveness and program improvement. Professional and education agencies that specialize in dual language and enrichment bilingual education also offer valuable information and data on what it takes to create a high-quality program. Based on all the information gathered, the next step is to determine program model, criteria, and goals that best suit the school's student and teacher population and its academic, linguistic, and cultural goals. Selecting the most suitable program for a particular school requires careful consideration of components most compatible with the school's existing organization, demographics, and philosophy (Soltero 2004).

Family and Community Participation in the Planning Stages

Families and the community contribute in significant ways to shaping and building sustainable dual language programs. For families to develop informed opinions and provide constructive input about dual language education in general and the school's program in particular, it is essential that they are invited to be part of decision making from the start. Families and other interested community members can participate in dual language school visits, information sessions, school-based discussions, and planning meetings.

While families of ELs are increasingly interested in enrolling their children in dual language programs, it is not unusual for some to still be opposed to L1 instruction for their children (Giacchino-Baker and Filler 2006). This rejection typically results from a lack of understanding of bilingual education (Baker 2014; Shin 2000). The most common reasons for rejecting bilingual education are fears that their children will not learn English, will not do well academically, and will experience discrimination and prejudice. Families are well aware that English proficiency is critical for better education and job opportunities. But they do not always understand that it is not necessary to lose the L1 in order to learn English, and that just speaking to their children at home in the LOTE will not develop academic and advanced literacy in the L1. Parents who are initially opposed to implementing dual language education at their school can become the most dedicated of supporters. This change of heart can come from being involved in the decision-making process and gaining better understandings about language acquisition and dual language education.

Mrs. Li and Mr. Bocca, two of the most involved parents at Sinfin Elementary School, were initially opposed to the idea of starting a dual language program at their school. Mrs. Li had three children in the general education program, twins in preschool, and one child in first grade. Although her family is of Chinese heritage, everyone in her house spoke only English. Mr. Bocca's family emigrated from Argentina only two years before, and everyone at home spoke only Spanish. Two of his children were in the transitional bilingual program, one in preschool and one in first grade. Mrs. Li and Mr. Bocca were troubled that the program being proposed was a two-way 80-20 model. Both parents were concerned, but for different reasons. Mrs. Li was worried that her twins would fall behind academically and not learn how to read and write in English. On the other hand, Mr. Bocca felt that his child would not develop English proficiency in a program that devoted so much time to Spanish.

Mr. Bocca and Mrs. Li raised their concerns on multiple occasions with the principal and teachers. In response, they were invited to participate in the planning committee, attended several information sessions, and visited two nearby dual language schools. While Mrs. Li and Mr. Bocca had a better understanding of the program goals and its structure after the school visits and information sessions, they were still not convinced. To offer more opportunities to learn about and discuss the program, the principal scheduled monthly parent meetings where their questions and concerns were addressed. Guest speakers with expertise in dual and bilingual education were invited to speak to the parents, along with dual language parents from the nearby dual language schools. The teachers also showed videos they found on the Internet highlighting successful dual language programs across the country. After extensive discussion and many questions, Mr. Bocca and Mrs. Li began to feel that the program would be beneficial for their children and would not impede their academic or English development. They knew that most teachers were very dedicated, used learner-centered instruction, were willing to invest time to plan, and were committed to supporting and including families. Once the program was launched, Mrs. Li and Mr. Bocca volunteered to lead the dual language parent council and participated in the dual language evaluation committee. After five years in the program, both parents were more than satisfied with their children's academic progress and impressed by their bilingual and biliterate skills. They grew into such advocates that they became the "dual language parent ambassadors" and volunteered each year to answer questions and respond to concerns from new parents.

Parents and community members that are selected to be part of the planning committee should include those who are active and involved in the school, like Mr. Bocca and Mrs. Li, and who embrace bilingualism and cultural diversity. Ongoing information sessions give families opportunities to share their views and contributions through face-to-face conversations. Giacchino-Baker and Filler (2006) found that for LOTE families, other parents were the major influence in enrolling their children in dual language education, while for native English parents the major influences were teachers and administrators.

Visit Existing Dual Language Programs

School visits should include both well-established and newer dual language programs. In newer programs, teachers and school leaders can offer ideas and perspectives about their experiences, all of which are still fresh in their minds, like how they involved families and the community, how they responded to teacher doubts and concerns, and where they found LOTE instructional materials. These schools are likely to still be adapting and fine-tuning their programs. Observing the actual day-to-day classroom practices of experienced dual language teachers and school leaders is also very valuable. Visiting an established dual language school can offer a good sense of specific program elements, how the school has adjusted to the needs of changing local and state mandates, and how the program has evolved during its time of implementation.

Professional Development

Participation in professional development sets the groundwork for making well-informed decisions and creating high-quality, sustainable programs. Beyond traditional workshops, opportunities for professional development can include conferences, university coursework, book studies, professional learning communities, peer observations, and networking with other dual language schools. Networking facilitates support and collaboration among teachers and school leaders across schools and districts. Regional and national conferences, such as La Cosecha and the Two-Way & Dual Language Immersion (TWDI) conferences, offer the most current information and research on dual language and related fields (see Appendix B for a list of dual language conferences). Professional development for dual language teachers and school leaders should extend beyond program development to include second language acquisition, biliteracy development, instructional approaches, cross-cultural curriculum, family involvement, and authentic assessment.

Professional development should not be limited only to those directly involved in the dual language program. Sustainability, especially in strand models, is often affected by the degree of understanding and support by the rest of the school staff. Consequently, everyone needs to participate in professional development about dual language, including support personnel like librarians, special education teachers, office staff, paraprofessionals, and those who teach specials (in elementary grades) and non-core content classes (in high school). Many schools have in-house experts that can be tapped to share their expertise. Teachers and school leaders with backgrounds in bilingual, ESL, and world language education can provide workshops and mentor teachers who are new to the program.

Writing a Plan of Action

Schools often develop a short-term plan but fail to create a long-term strategic plan that looks beyond the first years of implementation (see Figure 2-5). Failing to write a strategic plan may have negative consequences in the first years and may contribute to the demise of the program later on. A long-term plan involves adjustments for program improvement (program guidelines), areas that need to be updated (Dual Language Handbook and website), new elements (mentoring, biliteracy awards), and expansion (from elementary to high school, high school to college).

Vision and Mission Statements

School vision and mission statements "inspire and provide a sense of purpose and direction for the entire school community" (Soltero 2011, 41). Creating or revising the school's vision and mission statement to reflect dual language program goals can

Short-Term Plan of Action
Planning year and Year 1
- Select DL model
- Establish timetable
- Develop guidelines
- Create DL handbook
- Include program in school website
- Identify teachers
- Build schoolwide buy-in
- Plan/participate in professional development (PD)
- Adapt the curriculum
- Identify/purchase materials
- Create evaluation plan
- Conduct parent information sessions
- Create student recruitment plan

Long-Term Plan of Action
Year 2 and beyond
- Review guidelines and scheduling
- Update DL handbook and website
- Evaluate program
- Hire new bilingual teachers and staff
- Provide new teacher mentoring
- Identify master teachers
- Maintain school buy-in
- Check for cohesion and consistency
- Continue PD and professional learning communities (PLC)
- Create videos of exemplary teaching
- Establish a DL parent council
- Create biliteracy pathway recognitions
- Create a K–12 expansion plan
- Present program at conferences

FIGURE **2-5**
Short-Term and Long-Term Plans

be a challenging process. The difficulty comes from trying to develop a genuine and accurate representation of a school's collective beliefs without sounding formulaic, artificial, or overly ambitious. Vision and mission statements are best developed by involving all stakeholders in the school. This can be a sensitive process, because not all the staff may share the same beliefs and attitudes toward bilingual education or linguistic and cultural diversity. Nonetheless, this can be done by providing safe spaces to brainstorm ideas about shared principles of education and how the dual language program fits in that schoolwide philosophy.

The vision and mission statements should highlight language and cultural diversity as valuable assets and resources that strengthen students' views about themselves and others while increasing their academic success (Collier and Thomas 2014). The degree to which dual language is reflected in the vision and mission, especially for program strands, shows the extent of the school's commitment to the program. The vision and mission should be reader-friendly, written in both the LOTE and English (and any other languages spoken by the students in the school), and posted in prominent places around the school as well as school's website. Below are examples of concepts that can be considered when writing or revising the vision and mission statements to reflect the principles of dual language education:

- Celebrate and promote language diversity.
- Cultivate a love of learning languages and their respective cultures.
- Develop linguistic and cultural college and career readiness.
- Prepare students to fully function in a global society.
- Develop multiliteracies for the information age.
- Increase multilingual, cross-cultural, and digital/technology skills.
- Enhance innovation, creativity, and problem-solving competencies.

- Advance social, environmental, and civic responsibility.
- Strengthen intergroup connections.
- Advocate for language rights and linguistic equity.

The school vision should also serve to engage students in analysis and reflection about the purposes and advantages of being biliterate and to help them understand why they are in the dual language program. Students above third or fourth grade can research other dual language schools' visions and also analyze position statements from organizations like the American Council on the Teaching of Foreign Languages, National Association for Bilingual Education, or documents such as the Hague Recommendations on the Education Rights of National Minorities and the Language Policy Division of the Council of Europe. Students at Telpochcalli Dual Language Elementary in Chicago engaged in this type of reflection and analysis of their mission statement (see Figure 2-6).

FIGURE **2-6**
Telpochcalli Dual Language Mission Analysis by Students

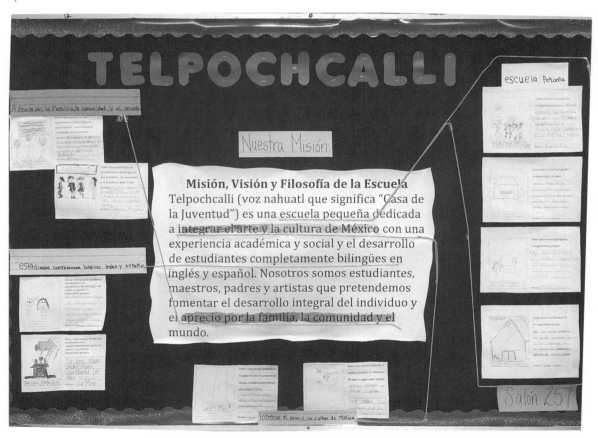

Inter-American Magnet School in Chicago, one of the oldest dual language elementary schools in the country, provides a good example of a vision that clearly reflects the tenets of dual language education.

> Inter-American Magnet School (IAMS) strives to promote academic excellence through bilingual and multicultural education. Spanish dominant, English dominant and bilingual speakers develop fluency and literacy skills in both languages. Through its dual language program, students affirm the values of their own cultures while acquiring an understanding, appreciation, and acceptance of other cultures and demonstrating social consciousness in a pluralistic world. At IAMS, a caring, cooperative and accepting school climate is fostered to promote the social, affective and cognitive development of the whole child, and in which parents are active partners in the formal schooling of their children. (IAMS 2013)

Timeline of Implementation

Implementation of new dual language programs needs to be gradual, starting with the lowest grade level (see Figure 2-7). For elementary programs, it is best to start with at least two grade levels—either PK–K or K–1—so that there is a larger group of teachers to share experiences, ideas, frustrations, and successes. In single-strand programs, beginning with just one kindergarten classroom makes that one teacher carry the program alone without the benefit of sharing experiences and having peer support. For middle and high schools, dual language students transitioning from dual language elementary schools, or others who are already biliterate, can participate in the program starting in the lowest grade and adding one grade level each subsequent year.

Program Year	Grade								
First Year	PK–K								
Second Year	PK–K	1st							
Third Year	PK–K	1st	2nd						
Fourth Year	PK–K	1st	2nd	3rd					
Fifth Year	PK–K	1st	2nd	3rd	4th				
Sixth Year	PK–K	1st	2nd	3rd	4th	5th			
Seventh Year	PK–K	1st	2nd	3rd	4th	5th	6th		
Eighth Year	PK–K	1st	2nd	3rd	4th	5th	6th	7th	
Ninth Year	PK–K	1st	2nd	3rd	4th	5th	6th	7th	8th

FIGURE **2-7**
Timeline of Implementation in Elementary Dual Language Programs

Starting a two-way program in all grades at once is not recommended, because students in the higher grades will not have sufficient command of the L2 to cope with the curriculum in both languages (Soltero 2004). This would be particularly challenging for English-dominant students who do not have L2 support at home or access to academic L2. As the first cohort of dual language students progresses through the program, one grade level is added each year. While this may seem obvious to many, some elementary schools have launched the program in all grades at once, such as the case at Dosul Elementary. With the district's promise of additional resources and a full-time bilingual teacher position, Gyeong—the principal at Dosul—was so eager to start the program that he decided to launch a schoolwide 50-50 two-way model in all K–6 grades. Within the first month, English-dominant students and their teachers in the upper grades were beside themselves trying to cope with the curriculum in Spanish. Parents soon joined the upper grade teachers and students, complaining that their English-dominant children, some of whom were monolingual English speakers, could not understand the content in Spanish and were receiving failing grades, especially in language arts and social studies. By mid-spring, a group of teachers and parents met with Gyeong and asked that the program be rolled back and implemented only in PK–1, adding a grade level each year after that. He agreed, but by that time the staff and parents had already began to sour on the idea of dual language education and the program ended after a few years. Two teachers who left to teach in another dual language school said that the program never stood a chance because Gyeong did not really understand dual language education, and there had been very little planning and almost no consultation with families and teachers. His primary motivation for starting the program had been the promise of additional resources for the school. What happened at Dosul Elementary is a cautionary tale against rushing into starting dual language education without a full understanding of what it takes to plan and implement.

Program Description and Programmatic Goals

Writing the description of the program helps to formulate clear and detailed explanations about the model and fine-tune those elements that may seem confusing to teachers or families. The program description should include the vision and mission statements, as well as organizational elements like scope (strand or whole school), language model (total or partial immersion), student language population (one-way or two-way), language of initial literacy instruction (sequential or simultaneous), and classroom organization (self-contained or team-teaching). The description should also include program goals. It is important to note the difference between dual language learning goals, which refer to student learning outcomes (biliteracy, academic, and cultural competencies) and programmatic goals, which speak to program implementation criteria. These goals are necessary for future program evaluation and needs-assessments, which will be further discussed in Chapter 6. Dual language programmatic goals may include the following criteria:

- Students stay in the program for at least six to eight years.
- The coordinator provides administrative and curricular support.
- Funding is allocated for the program each year.
- The school library increases bilingual/multicultural books each year.
- Educators attend professional development or conferences at least twice a year.
- Teachers meet at least twice a week for planning and sharing.
- Dual language parent meetings are offered once a month.

These types of explicit programmatic goals guide implementation and provide criteria for program evaluation. Goals may be added or modified each year, depending on school needs, changing demographics, or new district and state mandates.

Total or Partial Immersion Dual Language?

The question of whether to implement total or partial immersion is mostly relevant to elementary schools, since middle and high schools generally have a 50-50 language allocation. In elementary grades, research on dual language education points to total immersion as being more effective than partial immersion models in developing higher levels of LOTE proficiency and cross-cultural competencies (Lindholm-Leary 2001). However, not all schools have the necessary conditions to implement total immersion. The decision about which model to implement must be considered in light of the languages represented in the school, the level of family and school commitment, district and state policies, student mobility rates, access to certified bilingual teachers, and availability of LOTE instructional materials.

One critical factor that drives whether to implement a partial or total immersion model is the LOTE skills of the existing teaching staff, as well as access to qualified bilingual teachers. For schoolwide total immersion elementary models, most of the teachers must be bilingual in the primary grades. This has implications for existing teaching staff and prospective new hires. Another factor is student mobility. High mobility rates, where there are significant numbers of students coming and going, or practicing "circular mobility" (students regularly transferring in and out of the same school), negatively affect students' ability to sustain and develop biliterate skills. This is particularly problematic for native English speakers or English-dominant students in total immersion programs, because the majority of content instruction, and often literacy instruction, is conducted in the LOTE. The linguistic makeup of both teachers and students, as well as teacher and parent expectations for students' bilingual and biliterate development, all bear in the decision of whether to implement a total or a partial immersion model.

One-Way or Two-Way Dual Language Program?

Choosing to implement a one-way or two-way model depends largely on the community and student population (Soltero 2004). Because two-way programs have an equal or near-balanced number of LOTE and native English speakers, this model tends to be more effective in developing bilingualism and biliteracy as students interact for academic and social purposes in both languages (deJong 2004). Because students have a real and immediate purpose for communicating in the L2, the language acquisition process is more comprehensible, motivating, interesting, and purposeful. Students also become authentic language and cultural models for their peers. But when one language group dominates the classroom learning space, as discussed in Chapter 1, this opportunity is weakened, since students have less pressing needs to communicate in their L2, especially in the LOTE.

A considerable imbalance of students from each language background (few native speakers of the LOTE or English) creates challenges for two-way program teachers. Maintaining balanced numbers of students from both languages can be difficult, especially for neighborhood schools that are bound to their community's language demographics. A study of seven dual language programs conducted by Cortina, Makar, and Mount-Cors (2015) found that "Changes in the composition of the city neighborhoods generate challenges for enrollment and structure of dual language programs. While some of the schools have not been subjected to the problem of maintaining a program balance between the two languages, others were faced with the possibility of closing their programs altogether because they did not have enough Latino students" (10).

Attrition also affects this language balance and is especially problematic in elementary dual language strands that only have one classroom per grade level, as well as in middle and high schools. For example, a strand program in which the first cohort in PK or K starts with twenty-five children may have fewer than fifteen students left by fourth or fifth grade if the school has a high mobility rate. As previously mentioned, accepting new students in the program after second grade, particularly English-dominant students, is not a good idea because the curriculum becomes more demanding and less contextualized in third grade and beyond. Monolingual English-speaking students who enter the program in these grades would face difficulties understanding academic concepts in the LOTE. For middle and high school, there needs to be a critical mass of dual language students to fill courses.

School and Family Orientations

Schools with new programs often offer an orientation at the beginning of the first year, but this is not enough for families and staff to fully understand how the program works. At the very minimum, there should be two or three orientations for families and staff that include research on dual language education and the benefits of biliteracy; a description of the model, language allocation, and goals; a timeline for implementation; and other topics like funding, professional development, and assessment (see Figure 2-8).

Because schoolwide buy-in is so critical for program effectiveness and sustainability, having several orientations on dual language education for the entire staff is especially relevant. All school staff, from librarians, to fine arts teachers, to office clerks and custodial staff should have a good understanding of the program. While it would be impractical, and perhaps unnecessary, for every staff member to understand every single program in a school, understanding the basics tenets of dual language is necessary even when the school implements a strand. Unfortunately, it only takes a few misinformed staff members to undermine the program. The pervasiveness of misinformation regarding bilingualism and second language acquisition, especially for ELs, often weakens bilingual programs. This type of misinformation led the Rocha School Board, mentioned in Chapter 1, to initially vote against expanding dual language to middle school. Several Board members argued that bilingual instruction for ELs beyond the elementary grades was not necessary and could interfere with their progress in academic English. One Board member stated that continuing to offer L1 instruction, even to former ELs, would make them revert back to Spanish and use their L1 as a crutch. These types of common, but misguided, views must be countered by facts and research data.

> **Orientation Topics for Parents and School Staff**
> - Description (length, language allocation, resources, etc.)
> - Linguistic, academic, and cross-cultural goals
> - Key research that supports dual language and bilingualism
> - Basics of second language acquisition
> - Instructional approaches and assessments
> - Ways for families to support students' L2 at home

FIGURE **2-8**
Dual Language
Orientation Topics

Families unsure about having their children in dual language programs must also be given many opportunities to ask questions, voice their concerns, and discuss issues that are most relevant to them. If the school is moving from an existing transitional bilingual program to dual language, the differences between the two models need to be explained. Parents should understand what a dual language program is, as well as the basics of second language acquisition such as the difference between conversational and academic language, the time it takes to acquire the L2, and ways to support the L2 at home. A common fear, especially among EL families, is that their children will be confused by using two languages and will fall behind in acquiring English. To address these concerns, school staff should present research on the benefits of bilingualism and biliteracy, as well as the effectiveness of additive bilingual education. Particularly relevant are the latest brain research studies on cognitive advantages of bilingualism discussed in Chapter 4 (Bialystok 2011; Bialystok, Craik, and Luk 2012;

Costa and Sebastián-Gallés 2014). Inviting a guest speaker from a well-established dual language program or showing a short video of a high-quality program helps to create interest and build understanding. Appendix B offers a list of videos that are free and available on the Internet. Providing a short article that presents a "Dual Language 101" introduction to the program would also be helpful. Organizations like Dual Language Education of New Mexico and Internet sites like Colorín Colorado offer free online articles for teachers and families. Finally, it is worthwhile to create a list of frequently asked questions in the LOTE and English that can be posted on the school's website. Schools that have the technology know-how can create orientation webinars, short information videos, and other digital communication. Depending on parents' familiarity with technology, schools may need to offer workshops on how to use online resources and digital communication platforms.

Instructional Materials and Resources

The quality and availability of instructional materials in both languages are critical to program quality and effectiveness. These materials include a wide range of resources such as trade and reference books, periodicals, films, digital tools, online programs, technology, maps, music, instruments, manipulatives, artifacts, and visual aids like posters and signs. Concerns are sometimes raised that dual language education is more costly than other programs. In reality, it does not require any more or any fewer instructional resources than any other high-quality program. The only extra cost for bilingual and dual language programs is that most instructional materials need to be in both languages. This is the case for any other type of bilingual program that requires instructional materials in the LOTE and English, including specialized ESL materials.

Bilingual and Multicultural Children's and Young Adult Literature

An essential resource in dual language classrooms and school libraries is a collection of authentic books in the two languages. Because one of the three goals of dual language education is to develop cross-cultural competencies, multicultural literature is a critical component of its curriculum. Authentic multicultural children's and young adult literature offers interesting, captivating, and relevant topics full of rich and natural language. These types of books can be used to develop students' language and academic knowledge and expand their cross-cultural understandings. Banks (2015) suggests that literature is a powerful medium for understanding the world, because it can be a major carrier of multicultural concepts and ideologies. Authentic multicultural literature helps to develop cultural awareness and positive self-worth for both LOTE and native English speakers. Children's and young adult literature that accurately portrays the customs, values, beliefs, traditions, practices, and histories of various groups expands students' understandings of diversity and helps to reduce stereotyping and biases. Books that depict contemporary and historical experiences of diverse groups such as refugees, single-parent families, or people with disabilities provide expanded perspectives about diversity and a pluralistic society. Exposure to high-quality multicultural literature also helps students understand and embrace the distinctiveness of other ethnic groups, eliminate cultural ethnocentrism, and develop multiple perspectives.

In selecting multicultural children's and young adult literature, teachers must be aware of overt and covert biases found in the story or illustrations by looking for stereotypes. Many classic children's books that have negative or biased messages about women and other diverse groups are still in use today. For example, the classic *The Five Chinese Brothers* (Bishop and Weise 1939) portrays a common stereotype that all Chinese people look the same. The story begins with, "Once upon a time, there were five Chinese brothers and they all looked exactly alike." Portraying any group of people as one-dimensional reaffirms negative stereotypes. Some publishers sell multicultural curricular materials that on the surface appear inoffensive, but have many ethnic, cultural, or gender stereotypes. The most common are illustrations showing Mexicans wearing large *sombreros*, Japanese wearing *kimonos*, or Native Americans living in tepees. In contemporary life, most Mexicans and Japanese do not wear sombreros or kimonos and most Native Americans do not live in tepees.

Publishers have responded to the popularity of dual language programs by increasing their selections of bilingual books and digital resources, especially in Spanish and Chinese. There are also more available books about cultural diversity, the immigrant experience, and cross-cultural topics relevant for dual language education. Picture books that focus on contemporary immigrant experiences, such as *My Name Is Bilal* (Mobin-Uddin 2005), *One Day We Had to Run! Refugee Children Tell Their Stories in Words and Paintings* (Wilkes 2004), *Xochitl and the Flowers; Xochitl, la Niña y las Flores* (Argueta 2005), *La Mariposa* (Jiménez 2000), and *America Is Her Name* (Rodríguez 1998), are particularly appealing because of their authentic content and rich illustrations. School and classroom libraries should also have a variety of genres, including periodicals and digital resources. In the primary grades, patterned and predictable language books with cultural diversity themes like *Why Mosquitoes Buzz in People's Ears* (Aardema 1992), *The Pot That Juan Built* (Andrews-Goebel 2002), or *Abiyoyo* (Seeger 1998) provide literacy scaffolds to develop reading and writing skills in the LOTE and English. These books also offer rich authentic language that promotes vocabulary building and models of grammatical structures in the L2. Picture books with animal themes, familiar fairy tales, and songs help young bilingual learners to predict, infer, confirm/disconfirm prediction, and connect new information to their prior knowledge.

For middle and high schools, young adult books like *La Linea* (Jaramillo 2008), *The Circuit: Stories from the Life of a Migrant Child* (Jiménez 1997), *A*

Step from Heaven (Na 2003), *An Island Like You: Stories of the Barrio* (Ortiz Cofer 1996), and *The Brief Wondrous Life of Oscar Wao* (Díaz 2007) depict compelling storylines and characters that expand students' understandings of their own and others' immigrant experiences, which can be easily integrated into the social studies curriculum. Young adult books include longer and more sophisticated storylines, more low frequency words, and more complex sentence structures. Chapter books have fewer context cues like illustrations, so students can engage in pair and group reading and have many opportunities for discussions. Students—regardless of their ages—can also write their own reading materials in both languages. These student-authored LOTE or bilingual books create additional reading materials for instruction.

Designing effective and sustainable dual language programs requires deliberate and thoughtful planning that accounts for the needs and desired outcomes of students, their families, and all the school stakeholders. The planning year is a critical aspect of creating well-designed, high-quality programs because it is during this time that the school community becomes informed about which dual language model is best suited for the school.

Suggestions for Further Reading

Collier, Virginia P., and Wayne P. Thomas. 2009. *Educating English Learners for a Transformed World*. Albuquerque, NM: Fuente Press.

Hamayan, Else, Fred Genesee, and Nancy Cloud. 2013. *Dual Language Instruction from A to Z: Practical Guidance for Teachers and Administrators*. Portsmouth, NH: Heinemann.

Tedick, Diane, J., Donna Christian, and Tara Williams Fortune. 2011. *Immersion Education: Practices, Policies and Possibilities*. Buffalo, NY: Multilingual Matters. ✳

Dual Language Program Implementation

Neither the choice of program model nor the implementation of effective program features is a straightforward affair once we consider the local context and the decisions educators must make every day. The need for flexibility and responsiveness does not imply randomly designed approaches to schooling in diverse settings. Decision making that is not grounded in a coherent vision can easily fragment the schooling experience for students. . . . Responding to external pressures or changing circumstances may result in practices that are not aligned with what we know about effective schooling for multilingual learners.

—Ester de Jong, *Foundations of Multilingualism in Education*

Dual language education requires a comprehensive and well-articulated program design, so the first few years of implementation are particularly important in developing the strongest possible foundations for long-term success. While the first year of implementation puts into practice all the planning done the previous year, it also requires continued planning and adjustments to the program. In almost every case, modifications need to be made to certain program aspects that are not working quite as planned or that were not fully considered during the planning year. Schedules and language allocations almost always need to be modified as teachers try out different time distributions for each language. Many of the components planned the previous year require continued attention, such as ongoing teacher support and professional development, funding and resource allocation, and opportunities for collaborative planning and dialogue. School leaders in strand programs must look out for tensions that may arise if non-dual language teachers perceive they are not given the same type of resources and support as their dual language counterparts. Families need to continue to become informed, consulted, and given reassurances that their children are progressing academically and acquiring the L2. Parents and other family members also should receive guidance on how to support their children at home.

The First Year: What to Expect

La Coronilla Elementary, an urban PK–8 neighborhood school, offers a glimpse into the types of processes that teachers and principals experience in the first year of program implementation. At La Coronilla, the main motivation to create a dual language program was in response to improving their existing transitional bilingual program, so the idea was presented to the families and staff, who voted in favor of starting the program in K–1 the following year. Raquel, the kindergarten bilingual teacher, who had experience teaching in a dual language program at another school, was asked to take the role of program coordinator. She continued to be the kindergarten teacher for the first two years of the program, so Eloisa, the principal, paid her a stipend to work after school and also gave her two extra periods of preparation a week. Eloisa also allocated funds for instructional materials, teacher stipends for after-school and summer planning, and professional development.

After nearly a year of planning, the program began in all four K–1 classrooms. As coordinator, Raquel provided many types of support to parents and teachers. She organized monthly parent meetings and dual language teachers' bimonthly planning meetings and located instructional materials and professional development opportunities for the principal and teachers. Raquel also monitored student enrollment and classroom placement to ensure language balance in all classrooms. The K–1 teachers knew they could go to her with questions and also direct parents to speak to her about their concerns. Because the first year there were eight dual language teachers starting the program (four at each grade level) and because Raquel was available to address problems and support their needs, they did not feel as anxious and overwhelmed as they had anticipated. The teachers thought that Eloisa was instrumental in helping schedule time for them to continue planning and talk to each other. Even though the second-grade teachers were not yet in the dual language program that first year, they met frequently with K–1 teachers, attended professional development, and visited other dual language schools. The second-grade teachers also met after school and during the summer to plan and order instructional materials in preparation for the next year, when the first-grade dual language students would be moving to their grade level.

Toward the end of the first year, K–1 and second-grade teachers met to organize student placement for the next grade level and transfer student portfolios. Eloisa, Raquel, and the K–1 teachers also met to reflect on the challenges and successes of the first year and identified two priorities to work on the following year that had proved to be most challenging: scheduling and assessment. At the end of the year, teachers organized a Dual Language Celebration to highlight students' achievements, display their work, present their portfolios, and prepared a performance in both languages for the entire school. In retrospect, everyone agreed that the first year was quite challenging but very rewarding. In the second year of implementation, many of the steps taken in the first year were continued, but with a focus on creating stronger supports for students in their L2. During the third year, when the program reached third grade, several significant changes took place: Raquel became a full time coordinator, PK was added, the first program evaluation was conducted, and a Dual Language Leadership Team was created that included one teacher representative from each grade level, the coordinator, and the principal. By the fourth year, the program evaluation showed that students were progressing well, teachers had become confident at implementing dual language, and families were happy with the results. The trajectory of the first few years of implementation at La Coronilla shows the types of adjustments and improvements that come from continued planning and reflection.

For the Global Academy High School, the first few years of implementation proved to be quite challenging because the school had over 2,000 students who spoke several languages besides English. The idea to implement a dual language program originally came from a discussion that Artigas, the principal at Global Academy, had with Lucy, the principal from one of the two dual language elementary feeder schools. Lucy had implemented the program for eleven years, so she had two cohorts of her dual language students at Global Academy in ninth and tenth grades. Unfortunately, those students were not able to continue their biliteracy development because Global Academy only offered beginner and intermediate world language classes. After many meetings and discussions, Artigas and his leadership team concluded that they had the right conditions to implement a dual language program. The two elementary dual language feeder schools would provide enough students to fill courses that could be taught by the bilingual-endorsed math and social studies teachers, as well as several Spanish world language teachers. For the past two years, the district had been encouraging high schools to expand their world language and heritage language programs, so Artigas knew that creating a dual language program would be supported by central office administrators.

Artigas put together a dual language task force that included one of the assistant principals, the social studies and math bilingual teachers, and two Spanish world language teachers, who spent the planning year gathering information about secondary dual language programs, attending professional development, and figuring out the logistics of implementation and scheduling. They were well aware that the most challenging issues in implementing a dual language program at the high school level were scheduling, availability of bilingual-endorsed content teachers, and having a critical mass of dual language students to fill courses. The dual language task force spent considerable time collaborating with the two dual language elementary feeder schools to make projections about the number of dual language students that would likely enroll at Global Academy. Artigas and the assistant principal analyzed the Spanish language proficiencies of their own secondary student population to determine how many would be eligible to participate in the program. Global Academy had a number of former ELs who were high-functioning bilinguals, even though they had not participated in elementary dual language education. They also calculated the number of ELs who would need bilingual math and social studies the following year to see if they could offer special Spanish periods for the dual language students. After they gathered all the necessary information, the task force concluded that there would be enough students to fill a ninth-grade world history class and a Spanish literature class, but would not offer algebra in Spanish the first year because of the needs of newcomer ELs.

One challenge was to convince incoming dual language and other biliterate students to forgo their electives and instead choose the dual language courses. The task force collaborated with the world language department to create a track toward AP in an effort to incentivize students to stay in the program. Artigas and the leadership team also created a public relations campaign to increase the visibility of the dual language program and make bilingualism, as they said, "cool." They challenged students to a slogan contest, and the participants came up with catchphrases like "Biliteracy Rules," "Bilingual Power," "Dos Idiomas Valen Por Dos," and "¡Soy Bilingüe!" and posted them throughout the school and on their website. Teachers showed videos on bilingual brain research, created lists of careers that require biliteracy, and publicized the benefits of earning the Seal of Biliteracy to students and families. The concerted effort to raise the "coolness factor" of biliteracy and bilingualism took root at Global Academy as an attractive program for students.

The accomplishments in their first year of implementation for La Coronilla Elementary and Global Academy High School were in large part due to the extensive planning in the prior year and the high level of principal support and investment. These programs were successful because families, teachers, and school leaders not only laid the groundwork for success, but also continued to innovate and plan in the first years of implementation.

Enrollment and Placement Procedures

The first year requires continued planning that involves processes for admitting students to the program and for classroom or course placement. For students new to the school, dual language programs commonly use one of two enrollment processes: selective or open admissions. In selective admissions, usually in magnet schools, students are typically admitted through a lottery system. Because two-way programs need to maintain a balanced representation of the two languages and cultures, sometimes language and ethnic background criteria are used. Two-way models do not generally admit new monolingual English-speaking students beyond second grade, so the program must begin with a balanced number of students from each language. In strand models, parents of students who are not in the dual language program may be interested in having their children join the program. Decisions on whether to accept them may depend on their level of bilingual proficiency, as well as program needs to maintain balanced representation of the two languages and cultures. It is worth noting that some students come to school fully bilingual, proficient in English and the LOTE. Others may be heritage speakers with limited proficiency in the LOTE and so are considered native English speakers with background in the LOTE.

Maintaining a balanced representation of the two languages requires careful attention to students' language proficiencies and their classroom placement, particularly in two-way programs with multiple classrooms at each grade level. In addition, programs that use a sequential initial literacy approach in the primary grades, in which students learn to read and write first in their L1, need a system to determine the language group to which the students are assigned. The same applies to two-way team-teaching classrooms that need to maintain a balanced representation of LOTE- and English-dominant students, as well as distribution of balanced bilingual students between the two team-teaching classrooms. Determining students' L2 proficiency is not always straightforward. ELs who are recent arrivals to the United States are likely not proficient in English, but some may have had prior English instruction. In addition to facilitating student classroom placement, determining students' proficiency levels in each language provides information for various language groupings within the classroom.

The Home Language Survey (HLS) is the first step to identify students' eligibility for bilingual or ESL services. The HLS is a short questionnaire required by federal law that parents or legal guardians fill out when registering their children in a public school. It asks whether the child speaks a LOTE at home. When a LOTE is identified on the HLS, a language assessment is administered to determine English proficiency level. Some families choose to not indicate a LOTE is spoken at home because they do not want their children in bilingual or ESL classes, so the HLS is not always reliable.

While the HLS helps to identify if LOTEs are spoken at home, it does not indicate L2 proficiency levels, which is done later through a normed language proficiency test. In the meantime, it is helpful to get an immediate general sense of students' language proficiencies for initial placement. This can be done when the student first enrolls, through an informal conversation using a checklist like the one in Figure 3-1. This provides a very general idea of students' oral receptive and expressive proficiency in each language. The teacher should let students know that they can respond in any language they prefer, but encourage them to communicate in the L2. Worth noting is that when students respond in their L1, it does not mean that they do not have competence in the L2. Sometimes, students prefer to communicate in the L1 or are reluctant to reveal that they speak the L2. This was the case for Miguel, a kindergarten EL who, even though was at a low intermediate level in English, refused to speak Spanish in the classroom and only answered the teacher in his halting English. At such a young age, he had already developed "self-shame" about his language, his heritage, and even his own name, wanting to be called Michael instead of Miguel. School staff should also take into account that very young children tend to initially be shy and uncomfortable speaking to people they do not know, so language interviews and oral tests might not always produce reliable information. Speaking with family members about what languages their children use at home with their siblings and grandparents, for example, and how often they speak either of the languages, provides a more complete picture of students' language use. Commercial oral language assessment instruments that show students' level of L2 oral fluency, grammar, vocabulary, and listening comprehension can also be used. The Center for Applied Linguistics' Student Oral Proficiency Assessment, Early Language Listening and Oral Proficiency Assessment, and Oral Proficiency Exam include hands-on activities to determine students' command of each language.

Separation of the Two Languages

In the past decade, researchers in the field of bilingual education have turned their attention to whether the two languages should be kept strictly separate or be integrated during instruction. Some researchers caution that a rigid separation of the two languages is not as necessary or as desired as previously thought, and that allowing students to explore the two languages in more natural contexts may be more beneficial (Cummins 2008b). García (2009) advocates for a more flexible approach to the rigid separation of languages as a reflection of how bilinguals use their two languages

Name			Grade		L2		Date	

RECEPTIVE LANGUAGE (English E and Chinese C)   E   C

- Understands and responds to commands or questions   ☐   ☐
- Responds to commands or questions with gestures   ☐   ☐
- Responds to commands or questions with words/phrases   ☐   ☐

PRODUCTIVE LANGUAGE (English E and Chinese C)   E   C

- Uses one-word utterances   ☐   ☐
- Uses phrases with some errors   ☐   ☐
- Uses phrases with no errors   ☐   ☐
- Engages in extended conversation   ☐   ☐

Mark approximate language level on the bilingual continuum:

CLM   CLD   BB   ELD   ELM

> **CLM**—Chinese Language Monolingual   **ELM**—English Language Monolingual
> **CLD**—Chinese Language Dominant   **ELD**—English Language Dominant
> **BB**—Balanced Bilingual

☐ Cannot determine at this time

FIGURE **3-1**
Informal Language
Proficiency Level Checklist

in their everyday lives. de Jong (2011) argues that reducing this rigid language com-
partmentalization "enhances the learning process, affirms students' identities and af-
filiations, and bridges different languages and cultures. Using their entire repertoire,
including code-switching or translanguaging, is natural for bilinguals and serves specific communicative functions" (215). She adds, "Keeping the two languages separate
for instructional purposes is a highly artificial practice for bilingual individuals" (215).

The debate seems to have created two camps: those who believe that the languages do not need to be separated for instruction and those who believe they
should. I take a middle-ground position. On one hand, separation of the two languages is necessary for programmatic reasons and to ensure students develop academic LOTE. On the other hand, cross-linguistic understanding advances students'
metalinguistic skills that lead to higher levels of biliteracy and more nimble ways of
using the two languages, like students' code-switching to fill vocabulary gaps or for
creative communication and other academic purposes. In this book, I use the term
metabilingual to expand the concept of metalinguistic awareness to thinking about
and manipulating the interactions of the two languages. A more in-depth discussion

about the intersection of the two languages, cross-linguistic influence and metabilingual awareness will be further discussed in Chapter 4.

While advocates of language separation contend that teachers should not code-switch, we are usually open to students' code-mixing, especially for those who are in the process of becoming bilingual, as well as for making cross-linguistic connections. An area of concern for many teachers is the potential for developing unstable code-switching, where the two languages are used simultaneously with limited grammatical and morphological consistency. Code-switching is a natural progression of second language acquisition and a normal way of communicating among bilinguals, and therefore should not be devalued. The key point is that while teachers should not code-switch in the classroom, students are allowed to do so when they are at the L2 beginning and intermediate levels, or when using the two languages simultaneously for particular communication (like bilingual poems or dramatization) or academic purposes (such as cross-linguistic strategies like cognates and contrastive analysis). Because teachers are models of academic L2 for students, especially in one-way programs where the teacher is at first the only proficient speaker of academic English, they should avoid code-switching and translation.

Many dual language researchers and educators contend that without these linguistic boundaries for instruction, the two languages may not have equal time and will not result in the highest possible levels of academic language proficiencies, especially in academic LOTE. The separation of the two languages in bilingual and dual language education is necessary for several reasons. At a very practical programmatic level, deliberate separation of the two languages helps ensure the language distribution of the program model (50-50, 90-10, 80-20). With a more casual and natural use of the two languages in the classroom, there is no way for teachers to confirm the amount of time spent in each language. Over time, this could prove problematic for the integrity of the model and for students' academic bilingual and biliteracy outcomes. It is well documented in the literature, and anecdotally by dual language teachers, that both ELs and native English speakers in dual language programs typically shift to using more English and preferring it as early as third or fourth grade (Palmer 2007). Potowski (2007) found that by the time students in one two-way total immersion dual language program reached eighth grade, all had stronger English language proficiency than Spanish. Formal time allocations with established academic and social purposes for using the LOTE are needed to raise its status and that of its speakers. This is also necessary to ensure that English does not dominate classroom interactions as previously discussed in Chapter 1. In the middle and high school grades, this is even more challenging. In their research on high school dual language, de Jong and Bearse (2011) reported on the types of barriers students experienced in maintaining and continuing to develop academic Spanish: a significant decrease in amount of time for instruction in Spanish and reduced use of Spanish outside the classroom, the limited role of Spanish as a medium of instru[...] content areas, and a shift to learning about Spanish (heavy focus on gramma[...] than through Spanish language arts classes.

Options for Separating the Two Languages

The various options for separating the two languages for instruction depend [...] dual language model and the specific context of each school (see Figure 3-[...] self-contained elementary classrooms, the two languages can be separated by [...] content, and/or thematic topic. Options for the separation of the two langu[...] by time include teaching mornings in one language and afternoons in the partner language, alternating days between the two languages, with Fridays alternating every other week, alternating languages every two days, or alternating entire weeks. Self-contained bilingual teachers can also alternate the languages by content or themes: one content area in one language and another content area in the partner language per quarter, semester or year. Certain thematic topics can also be used in assigning the two languages for instruction, especially when considering the availability of instructional materials. For example, a thematic unit on the United States Civil War might be best done in English while a thematic unit on the Spanish Conquistadores could be done in Spanish. In total immersion (80-20 and 90-10), all content areas are taught in the LOTE in PK–1 or second grades with ESL and some language arts in English. However, as the two languages reach equal balance for instruction in fourth grade and above, separation of the two languages can follow any of the options outlined here.

FIGURE **3-2**
Separation of the Two Languages

Teacher
- One teacher uses the LOTE and the other teacher uses English.

Time
- Teach mornings in LOTE and afternoons in English.
- Alternate languages every other day, or every two days.
- Alternate languages every other week or month.

Place
- One classroom uses the LOTE exclusively and the other uses English.
- Special classes (i.e., art, PE) have a designated language.
- Other spaces (i.e., library, lunchroom) have a designated language.

Content
- One or more content areas are taught in LOTE and the others in English.
- Alternate years for content exclusively taught in one language.

Theme
- Certain thematic units correspond to one or the other language (i.e., Maya and Incas in Spanish, the U.S. Civil War in English).

In self-contained primary classrooms, it is also helpful to have some system for when the teacher switches between the two languages—like an object (a scarf or a hat), a gesture (a switching motion like turning a knob), a saying (*uno dos tres inglés otra vez*), an image, or a sign—so that students and teachers differentiate the transition and time for each language (see Figure 3-3). In addition, systems for motivating students to use the LOTE, especially in third grade and above, can be done through cooperative-learning type rewards or incentives. Cooperative learning, which will be further discussed in Chapter 5, provides the optimum context for students to use academic language among each other in meaningful and consistent ways and already has an integrated reward system.

For team-teaching, the separation can happen by time, content, theme, teacher, and/or classroom. In team-teaching, the bilingual teacher uses the LOTE for instruction and the partner teacher (either monolingual English or bilingual) uses English. Time, content, or theme can follow the same options described above. For example, in a Japanese-English dual language program, one classroom is entirely in Japanese and the other entirely in English. Students typically move between the two classrooms alternating by time of the day, every other day, or every other week. Instruction for students in PK–2 is best provided in both languages within the week, preferably every other day or every two days. While there are a few successful partial immersion programs that separate the two languages for instruction by week in grades PK–2 (one week in LOTE and one week in English), it is best for students at this age to have opportunities during the week to learn in both their L1 and L2. Students in the early grades who are not yet proficient in the L2 and are beginning to develop academic language in their L1 should have daily access to the two languages.

FIGURE **3-3**
Visual Aids for Separating the Two Languages

Instruction in the students' L1 also provides scaffolds for them when they are learning difficult or unfamiliar content in the L2.

A Few Words About Translation

Using direct translation to help students understand lessons in the L2 is problematic on several fronts. First, if teachers translate, students are likely to tune out the L2 because they know they will eventually hear the messages in their L1. This reduces students' effort and motivation to develop the L2, especially in the LOTE for native English speakers. Second, translations take time away from instruction so the curriculum cannot be fully covered, because parts of the lessons are repeated in the students' L1. In other words, having to translate lessons and instructions chips away at the time that would be devoted to covering the curriculum. Translations of lessons or instructions may appear to take a few minutes here and there, but this accrues over time. Third, because instructional translations are not word-for-word, they become a weak summary of content and concepts. While teachers should not translate lessons or instructions, students can engage in translation as a tool for their own cognitive and metabilingual processing. Balanced bilingual students can also translate for other students, giving them opportunities to develop deeper understandings of the concepts they are translating. When students translate, they are paraphrasing and summarizing what is understood in one language into the other language, so teachers should explain that this is a high-order cognitive skill. Caution must be taken, though, not to ask bilingual students to translate entire lessons or concepts that they do not yet know or understand. Also, not all bilingual students enjoy translating, since many of them often engage in this "language brokering" on behalf of their families. In these cases, teachers can incentivize bilingual students to translate as part of cross-linguistic connection activities (further discussed in Chapter 4).

Raising the Status and Use of the LOTE in the School

English is clearly the language that holds the highest status in United States, and so it is particularly important for dual language programs to elevate the status of the LOTE in and outside the classroom. Creating a positive bilingual environment where all stakeholders see, hear, and use the LOTE alongside English helps to increase the value of the LOTE and give a more meaningful purpose for being bilingual and biliterate. One way to accomplish this is to have school signage in both languages throughout the school—for example, signs for the office, library, and auditorium should be in both languages. There should also be ample displays of students' work in the LOTE in school halls. Assemblies and award ceremonies should use the LOTE, and performances and school events should represent LOTE cultures. Often overlooked is the school website, which needs to provide as much information as possible in both languages. School libraries, especially in strand models, should make long-term plans to increase their holdings by allotting part of their budget to purchasing bilingual and multicultural books and multimedia, as well as authentic LOTE materials. Inviting speakers and performance artists, as well as organizing events, fairs, and exhibits that reflect the LOTE and its cultures increase their appreciation and value. Maintaining an equal status of the LOTE in relation to English is not an easy task, but one that needs ongoing attention and effort.

It is not unusual for dual language students to start losing interest in using the LOTE starting in third or fourth grade. Teachers and parents find it increasingly difficult to motivate them to use it as they move up the grades. To respond to this common problem, dual language programs and teachers must have explicit and comprehensive methods to encourage the use of the LOTE. Expectations to use the LOTE during certain times and for particular purposes need to be clear and enforced. While students who are at the beginner and low-intermediate levels of L2 proficiency should not be forced to use the L2, they need to be encouraged and incentivized to do so. Intrinsic motivations come from purposeful use of the LOTE, such as communication with pen pals, family, and community members who do not speak English. Students who understand the benefits of bilingualism and the effort that it takes to become biliterate can also be tapped to motivate others' use of the LOTE. Not surprising, students tend to prefer extrinsic motivation, so rewards, contests, and recognitions like the Seal of Biliteracy pathways awards can also be used. Displaying printed LOTE extensively across the school and in the school website, like in the Global Academy High School, as well as using it for announcements and assemblies, helps to elevate its status and purpose. Students can also be challenged to generate bilingual products like books, poetry, songs, pottery, or projects like designing a bilingual webpage or advertising campaign, creating and performing bilingual raps, rai or reggaetton, and writing bilingual plays or skits. In addition, interacting with authentic LOTE resources like LOTE newspapers, magazines, Internet sites, radio, and television increases bilingual students' interest and motivation.

Scheduling and Language Distribution

Undoubtedly, scheduling is one of the most challenging elements of dual language programming, since this often requires adjustments to maintain appropriate language allocation. Accounting for the time students spend in each language is critical to support the central premise of dual language education: development of biliteracy and academic language development of the LOTE. Because English very quickly becomes the preferred language for students in the United States, high levels of biliteracy and academic LOTE will not be achieved without sufficient academic engagement with the LOTE across grade levels. Periodic schedule checks are necessary to ensure cohesion and consistency in language allocation. For middle and high school programs, each dual language student needs to be tracked to ensure he or she is receiving the appropriate number of periods in the LOTE. In elementary grades, checking that the language distribution reflects the model can be done through a *language allocation count*. For example, a 90-10 dual language kindergarten class that has a daily forty-five-minute period of English instruction is close to the intended ninety percent LOTE time and ten percent English time during the week. On the other hand, if students spend additional five 50-minute periods a week in music and art classes in English, then the actual amount of time in the LOTE is reduced to seventy-seven percent and the amount of English is increased to twenty-three percent. In this scenario, the program is no longer implementing a 90-10 model, but closer to an 80-20 model. Counting instructional minutes may seem to be artificial and restrictive, but it is necessary to ensure the language allocation correlates to the model's language distribution.

`While individual teachers' schedules are periodically modified, the model language allocation should not be changed. If teachers do not follow the language allocation of the program model, there are serious consequences for students and their teachers as they move up the grade levels. For example, in an 80-20 model where the first-grade classroom is expected to have eighty percent of instructional time in the LOTE and twenty percent in English, a teacher who arbitrarily decides to teach sixty percent in the LOTE and forty percent in English will negatively affect students as they go up the grades. The immediate negative effects will be felt in second grade and by the second-grade teacher, who is expected to teach in the LOTE seventy percent of the time. As these students move up the grades, the LOTE proficiency becomes weakened, creating difficulties for them to cope with an increasingly demanding curriculum. Families and teachers are sometimes frustrated when students, especially native English speakers, do not make sufficient progress in the L2. Insufficient time in their L2 is often to blame.

At Maria Elena Walsh Elementary School, a 50-50 Spanish-English two-way dual language program, the lack of monitoring the language allocation became an unexpected problem. At the beginning of the fourth year of implementation, a few African American parents complained at a Dual Language Parent Advisory Committee meeting that their children could hardly string two sentences together in Spanish after being in the program for three years and were having increasing difficulty with the third-grade content textbooks in Spanish. These concerns were brought to the Dual Language Leadership Team, who tried to figure out what was causing this issue. After several meetings and much discussion, they realized they had two structural problems. First, they did not have a consistent way to assess the LOTE as a second language (LOTE-SL) for native English speakers; and second, they had not done a language allocation count of their schedules since the first year of implementation.

For the latter problem, grade-level teachers met with Luifer, the coordinator, to plot out their schedules with the language allocation and then count the weekly minutes for each language group. Luifer quickly discovered that while the Spanish-dominant students were receiving close to the 50-50 allocation, the English-dominant students were only receiving three hundred minutes of the total 1,800 weekly minutes in Spanish, amounting to less than twenty percent of the week in their L2. The teachers were very surprised to find this big discrepancy because they thought the language allocation was pretty close to the 50-50 mark for all students, and realized that just indicating the language of instruction in their weekly schedule did not actually show the time each language group was spending in the LOTE and in English. Because they were doing sequential literacy instruction and all the specials were in English, they also realized they had to account for the minutes for Spanish-dominant and English-dominant students separately. They adjusted the schedule to reflect a more balanced distribution of instructional time in English and LOTE, and by the end of the year the native English-speaking students were using and understanding the LOTE much more than before. After that, Luifer and the teachers calculated the language allocation count at the beginning of each year and periodically checked to ensure a balanced use of each language for instruction and learning.

As far as not having a system to assess the LOTE-SL for native English speakers, Luifer together with the Dual Language Leadership Team reviewed several Spanish assessment tools to see which would be the best fit for their needs. They chose a standardized language assessment that paralleled that of the state-required English language assessment given to ELs, which provided the same five levels of proficiency for listening, speaking, reading, and writing. While administering the language

FIGURE **3-4**
Two-Way Sample Schedule First Grade 50-50 English-Spanish Sequential Literacy

Grade _1_	Language Distribution _50-50_		Team-Teaching ☑	Self-Contained ☐		
Time	Subject		Spanish-Dominant Students		English-Dominant Students	
			Spanish	English	Spanish	English
8:00–8:20	Arrival—SSR, journals, shared reading, etc.	S	100		100	
8:20–9:50	Language arts integrated with social studies Reading, writing, oral language, vocabulary	E or S	450			450
9:50–10:20	L2 centers	E or S		150	150	
10:20–11:00	ESL and LOTE as a SL	E or S		200	200	
11:00–12:00	Math	E E S S S	150	150	150	150
12:00–12:45	Lunch and recess	E				
12:45–1:30	Specials	E E E E S	45	180	45	180
1:30–2:30	Science/social studies (alternate month)	E E S S S	180	120	180	120
2:30–3:00	Shared reading, journals, dismissal	E E S S S	75	75	75	75
TOTAL			Sp 1000	En 875	Sp 900	En 975
Note: Multiply daily minutes by 5 (days) Total minutes in a week = 1875						

proficiency test to English-dominant students added an additional layer of testing that teachers had to do, the data provided valuable information for instruction and monitoring students' progress in the LOTE-SL.

With the coordinator's help, teachers need to monitor if the time students spend in each language corresponds to the established language allocation of the model (total or partial immersion) or grade level (language distribution varies in total immersion models according to grade level). Specials such as art, music, or library must be included in the language allocation count, and whenever possible, should be offered in the LOTE. Typically in elementary grades, calculating the language allocation is based on the total number of minutes in a week. For example, a seven-hour school day has 420 minutes. If the forty-five minutes of lunch and recess are deducted, the daily minutes total 375, which are multiplied by five days for a total of 1,875 instructional weekly minutes. This can also be the baseline for programs that allocate the two languages every other week or separate the languages by quarter or theme. Figure 3-4 shows a sample schedule in a team-teaching first grade 50-50 two-way model with sequential literacy instruction. Figure 3-5 shows a sample of a self-contained first grade in a 50-50 two-way model, also with sequential literacy instruction. Both samples show that the language distribution is not exactly equal for each language group, a common outcome since an exact balance is difficult to accomplish.

FIGURE **3-5**
One-Way Sample Schedule: First Grade 50-50 English-Spanish Sequential Literacy

Grade_1_____ Language Distribution_50–50_____		Team-Teaching ☐ Self-Contained ☑	
Time	**Subject**	**Spanish-Dominant Students Language of Instruction**	
		Spanish	**English**
8:00–8:20	Arrival—SSR, journals, shared reading, etc. S	100	
8:20–9:50	Language arts integrated with social studies Reading, writing, oral language, vocabulary	450	
9:50–10:20	ESL centers E		150
10:20–11:00	ESL E		200
11:00–12:00	Math E/S	150	150
12:00–12:45	Lunch and recess E/S		
12:45–1:30	Specials E/S	45	180
1:30–2:30	Science/social studies (alternate month) E/S	150	150
2:30–3:00	Shared reading, journals, dismissal E/S	75	75
TOTAL		Sp 970	En 905
Note: Multiply daily minutes by 5 (days) Total minutes in a week = 1875			

Figure 3-6 represents a sample schedule in a self-contained second grade 80-20 two-way model where the language allocation at that grade is seventy percent French and thirty percent English. Figure 3-7 shows the same, but in a self-contained 80-20 model. Both samples show that the language distribution does not exactly correspond to the 70-30 allocation, but is close to what it should be.

In middle and high school programs, the separation of the two languages happens by content area teacher or by time in one of two scenarios. For example, in an Arabic-English dual language program, the bilingual math teacher instructs in Arabic and the science teacher in English, or the bilingual math teacher instructs half the time in Arabic and half the time in English. When one bilingual teacher instructs students in both languages, this typically happens either by quarter or semester. In the case of middle and high school, it is assumed that all participating students have high academic levels of proficiency in both languages, and therefore students are able to cope with the language demands of the curriculum without falling behind or feeling lost.

FIGURE **3-6**
Two-Way Sample
Schedule: Second Grade
80-20 English-French

Grade _2_ Language Distribution _70-30_		Team-Teaching ☐ Self-Contained ☑			
Time	**Subject**	**French-Dominant Students**		**English-Dominant Students**	
		French	**English**	**French**	**English**
8:00–8:20	Arrival—SSR, journals, shared reading, etc. F	100		100	
8:20–10:20	Language arts integrated with social studies E or F Reading, writing, oral language, vocabulary	400	200	400	200
10:20–11:00	ESL and LOTE as an SL E or F		200	200	
11:00–12:00	Math F	300		300	
12:00–12:45	Lunch and recess				
12:45–1:30	Specials E E E E F	45	180	45	180
1:30–2:30	Science/social studies (alternate month) F	300		300	
2:30–3:00	Shared reading, journals, dismissal F	150		150	
TOTAL		Fr 1295	En 580	Fr 1495	En 380
Note: Multiply daily minutes by 5 (days) Total minutes in a week = 1875					

The master schedule in high schools presents challenges that require careful attention to factors like teacher credentials (bilingual and content), critical mass of biliterate students so that there is class-size equity, and reducing the amount of tracking that may follow dual language students. The best candidates for middle and high school dual language programs are students who are biliterate and attended dual language and/or bilingual education programs in elementary school. Newcomers to the United States who have biliterate skills in English and the LOTE can also participate. As much as possible, dual language middle and high school programs should have a 50-50 language distribution, but this is often difficult to accomplish because of scheduling and access to bilingual content area teachers. Educators from the Ysleta Independent School District in El Paso, which offers one of the largest numbers of middle and high school dual language programs in the country together with the Center for Applied Linguistics and Dual Language of New Mexico, have drafted non-negotiables for middle and high school dual language programs (see Figure 3-8).

FIGURE **3-7**
One-Way Sample
Schedule: Second Grade
80-20 English-French

Grade 2 Language Distribution 70–30		Team-Teaching ☐ Self-Contained ☑	
Time	**Subject**	**French-Dominant Students Language of Instruction**	
		French	**English**
8:00–8:20	Arrival—SSR, journals, shared reading, etc. F	100	
8:20–10:20	Language arts integrated with social studies F Reading, writing, oral language, vocabulary	600	
10:20–11:00	ESL E or F		200
11:00–12:00	Math E E E F F	210	90
12:00–12:45	Lunch and recess E		
12:45–1:30	Specials E E E E F	45	180
1:30–2:30	Science/social studies (alternate month) F	300	
2:30–3:00	Shared reading, journals, dismissal F	150	
TOTAL		Fr 1405	En 470
Note: Multiply daily minutes by 5 (days) Total minutes in a week = 1875			

FIGURE **3-8**
Middle and High School
Non-Negotiables

Middle School Non-Negotiables	High School Non-Negotiables
• Required to take language arts in the LOTE from 6th–8th, in addition to another core content course in the LOTE each year from 6th–8th • Strict separation of languages for instruction—100% of class taught in the LOTE • K–12 commitment	• A minimum of eight credits in the LOTE over the course of 9th–12th, with a minimum of four credits in core content areas in the LOTE • Strict separation of languages for instruction—100% of class taught in the LOTE • K–12 commitment

Students in middle and high school dual language programs must take one period of language arts in the LOTE, one period of language arts in English, one or two periods of core content in the LOTE, and if possible, one or two periods of an elective in the LOTE. In a seven-or eight-period day, having only language arts and one content in the LOTE amounts to less than thirty percent of courses in the LOTE. Figure 3-9 presents a general idea of what a course schedule might look like, provided that there are sufficient bilingual content area teachers. In the sample below, each grade level has language arts periods in Spanish and in English, as well as one content area.

FIGURE **3-9**
Middle and High School
with a 50-50 Language
Allocation

	6th grade	7th grade	8th grade	9th grade	10th grade	11th grade	12th grade
1	Sp. LA	Sp. LA	Sp. LA	Sp. Writing & Grammar	Sp. LA & World History	IB/AP Sp. Literature	IB/AP Sp. Literature
2	En. LA	En. LA	En. LA	En. 1	En. 2	En. 3	En. 4
3	En. Math	Sp. Math	Sp. Math or Algebra	En. Algebra 1 or Geometry	En. Algebra 2 or Geometry	Sp. Trigonometry or P-Calculus	Sp. P-Calculus or Calculus
4	Sp. Science	En. Science	En. Science	Sp. Earth Science	En. Biology	Sp. Chemistry	En. Physics
5	Sp. Social Studies	Sp. Social Studies	En. Social Studies	Sp. World Geography LOTE focus	Sp. World History LOTE focus	En. US History	En. Economics or Psychology
6	En. PE	En. PE	En. PE	En. PE	En. PE	En. PE	En. PE
7	En. Fine Arts	En. Fine Arts	Sp. Fine Arts	En. Fine Arts	Sp. Fine Arts LOTE focus	En. Fine Arts	Sp. Fine Arts LOTE focus
8				En/Sp Elective	En/Sp Elective	En/Sp Elective	En/Sp Elective

While content delivery alternates between the two languages in 50-50 programs, and fourth grade and above in total immersion models, the curriculum is not repeated in both languages or translated. Rather, instruction of content is presented in a spiral approach by building on what was previously learned in the partner language. For instance, students studying the water cycle learn about *evaporation* in one language one day and about *condensation* in the partner language the next day, and so on. Figure 3-10 illustrates how the curriculum is covered by alternating the two languages but not repeating the content.

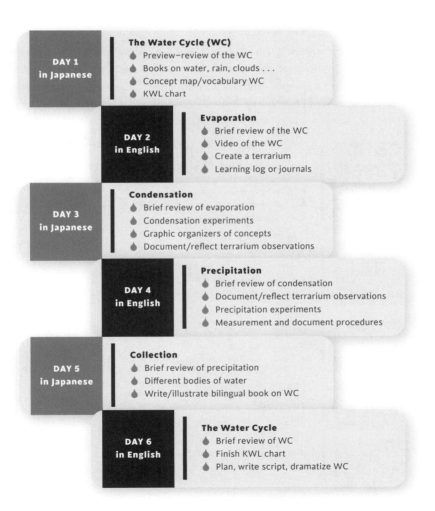

DAY 1 in Japanese

The Water Cycle (WC)
- Preview–review of the WC
- Books on water, rain, clouds . . .
- Concept map/vocabulary WC
- KWL chart

DAY 2 in English

Evaporation
- Brief review of the WC
- Video of the WC
- Create a terrarium
- Learning log or journals

DAY 3 in Japanese

Condensation
- Brief review of evaporation
- Condensation experiments
- Graphic organizers of concepts
- Document/reflect terrarium observations

DAY 4 in English

Precipitation
- Brief review of condensation
- Document/reflect terrarium observations
- Precipitation experiments
- Measurement and document procedures

DAY 5 in Japanese

Collection
- Brief review of precipitation
- Different bodies of water
- Write/illustrate bilingual book on WC

DAY 6 in English

The Water Cycle
- Brief review of WC
- Finish KWL chart
- Plan, write script, dramatize WC

FIGURE **3-10**
Alternating Languages by Day

Dual Language Program Teacher Handbook

A handbook for teachers and school leaders provides written guidelines needed for program cohesion and consistency (see Figure 3-11). Many of the elements in the school's dual language program handbook have already been addressed in the action plan during the planning year and revised during the first year of implementation. These include the vision and mission statements, program model description, goals, non-negotiables, instructional materials, admission/placement procedures, and scheduling. The handbook also includes the Dual Language Leadership Team as well as the types of supports the program coordinator provides (both discussed in more detail in Chapter 6). A frequently asked questions section for teachers can also be helpful.

Because constructivist and learner-centered approaches are more effective than direct instruction and rote learning in dual language education, it is particularly useful to include brief descriptions of these types of instructional practices, scaffolds, and cross-linguistic strategies. Resources and instructional materials such as culturally relevant texts and technology, links to content and L2 standards, and links to

FIGURE **3-11**
Dual Language Program
Teacher Handbook

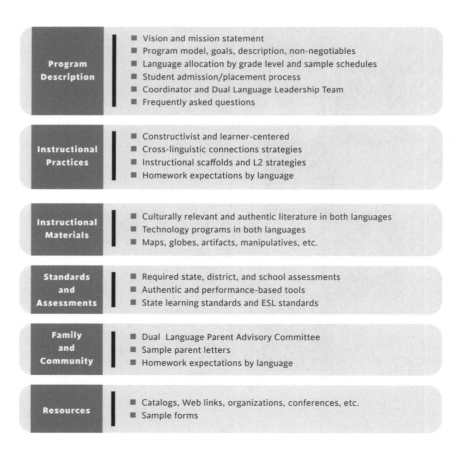

Program Description
- Vision and mission statement
- Program model, goals, description, non-negotiables
- Language allocation by grade level and sample schedules
- Student admission/placement process
- Coordinator and Dual Language Leadership Team
- Frequently asked questions

Instructional Practices
- Constructivist and learner-centered
- Cross-linguistic connections strategies
- Instructional scaffolds and L2 strategies
- Homework expectations by language

Instructional Materials
- Culturally relevant and authentic literature in both languages
- Technology programs in both languages
- Maps, globes, artifacts, manipulatives, etc.

Standards and Assessments
- Required state, district, and school assessments
- Authentic and performance-based tools
- State learning standards and ESL standards

Family and Community
- Dual Language Parent Advisory Committee
- Sample parent letters
- Homework expectations by language

Resources
- Catalogs, Web links, organizations, conferences, etc.
- Sample forms

curriculum aligned to these standards should also be included. For assessment, a comprehensive handbook outlines mandated state and/or district standardized tests as well as a list with brief descriptions of authentic and performance-based assessments, like portfolios, learning logs, and observational protocols. Other information might include resources on how to support families, increase parent participation, engage in community outreach, and helpful Internet links. Schools may consider developing an online, password-protected handbook that is easier to update and access.

Family Involvement and Participation

Family-school partnerships involve ongoing two-way communication where families share concerns, needs, expectations, and their cultural backgrounds. In turn, the staff help families to navigate school culture and norms and provide information and resources. Families should understand that becoming fluent in the L2 is a long-term process requiring their children to stay in the program for at least six to eight years. Families should also be aware of the types of personnel, resource, and time investments the school and district make to provide the highest-quality programs. This type of interaction breaks from the typical one-way communication that usually goes from school to home. A letter of commitment signed by both the parents and the school staff represents a symbolic formal agreement between families and the school, committing to work together to provide the necessary support for students to become biliterate, achieve academically, and develop strong cross-cultural competencies. Figure 3-12 describes the type of language that could be included in a school-family letter of commitment.

<table>
<tr><td>SCHOOL COMMITMENTS</td></tr>
</table>

The school staff agree to:
- provide quality additive education in two languages
- offer the dual language program for at least six years
- offer ongoing information and updates about the dual language program
- engage families and community in all aspects of the dual language program
- provide parent training, language classes, and other supports
- celebrate students' language and academic accomplishments

<table>
<tr><td>PARENT COMMITMENTS</td></tr>
</table>

I _____ agree to:
- keep my child in the dual language program for six years
- ensure my child has high attendance
- continue the development of my child's native language at home
- support my child's academic, language, socioemotional, and cross-cultural development
- attend monthly dual language parent meetings
- become involved in the classroom/school functions and events
- advocate for and support the dual language program

FIGURE **3-12**
Letter of Commitment: Some Suggestions for Inclusion

Families play a vital role in creating positive attitudes that promote and reinforce bilingualism in everyday activities at home. Sometimes, however, there is a mismatch between traditional expectations of school about the role of the family in their children's education and the family's ideas of what parent involvement means (Valdés 1997). Teachers and school leaders usually think of parent involvement in terms of observable activities like volunteering in the classroom, helping with homework, fund-raising, and attending meetings. However, EL families are often unfamiliar or not entirely comfortable with these conventional expectations for parent involvement. Jeynes (2005) found that traditional aspects of parent involvement were not as significant as the more indirect types of family support, like having high expectations for their children and creating a supportive home environment. Arias and Morillo-Campbell (2008) argue, "Non-traditional models of EL parental involvement are based on developing a reciprocal understanding of schools and families. These relationships situate the cultural strengths of family and community within the school curriculum, parental education, and parent advocacy" (11).

The school-home mismatch can be significantly reduced when schools integrate students' language and cultural practices as well as the knowledge and resources found in the home and community. When these *funds of knowledge* are used in the classroom, not only are schools capitalizing on students' experiences, but they are also validating their sociocultural backgrounds as assets to be tapped for academic learning (Moll and González 2004). For Mrs. Reid, a native of Jamaica, being invited to share her knowledge and experiences was as rewarding and educational for her and her children as it was for the school. Mrs. Reid's two children had been in two-way dual language since kindergarten. Her son was now in fifth grade and her daughter in second grade. She first became a parent volunteer and later a parent dual language representative in the Local School Council. From the beginning, she was a very committed supporter of the program, so she was asked to be part of the *Bienvenidos/Welcome Wagon*, made up of a group of parents who greeted new dual language families and students. They provided information, answered questions, and guided tours of the school to new parents and other visitors.

When Mrs. Reid's son Horace was in second grade, the teacher invited families to her classroom to share their expertise, talents, and experiences. Mrs. Reid volunteered to introduce students to Jamaican culture, customs, food, and music. The presentation was so well received that it extended into a full-blown thematic unit on the Caribbean. Mrs. Reid and the teacher collaborated in creating meaningful and interesting learning activities as students engaged in this thematic unit in English and Spanish. The students and the teacher learned about influential Jamaicans like Bob Marley and Colin Powell, Jamaican traditions, foods, music, and dance, as well as science topics related to the Caribbean islands, like habitats and wildlife. For

Horace, it was a great opportunity to learn more about his roots and feel proud of his heritage. Mrs. Reid shared her experience in her son's classroom with other parents, and soon teachers and families began to collaborate on similar projects. Prompted by the project's success, the third-grade teacher invited parents to participate in a thematic unit on urban habitats and recruited two fathers who worked in the construction business.

Dual Language Program Parent Handbook

Most schools have parent handbooks that include typical information like school and district policies, code of conduct, attendance, and the school calendar. Because the dual language program often gets lost in all of this information, a separate handbook dedicated to the program is needed. A dual language parent handbook should be easy to read and follow, have pertinent information on dual language relevant to families, be written in both languages, and offer tips for families to support their children's biliteracy and cross-cultural development. Elements to include in a dual language parent handbook are outlined in Figure 3-13.

Dual Language Family Council

For home-school partnerships to be effective, schools should facilitate participation of families in shared decision-making and leadership roles. A Dual Language Family Council can foster this type of engagement, especially for EL families, creating opportunities for self-empowerment and a deeper sense of ownership in their children's education (Soltero 2011). This type of parent council should have a clearly defined purpose with guidelines or bylaws that explain, for example, frequency of meetings and how they are conducted, how decisions are made, and members' scope of responsibilities. While this level of formality may not seem necessary, formalizing the council in this way is beneficial for several reasons: it establishes a clear purpose, creates a sense of ownership and importance, and reduces potential tensions among members. Having a formal structure also provides valuable experiences for parents to develop organizational and leadership skills.

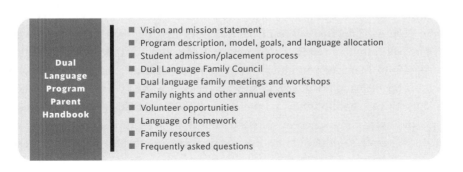

Dual Language Program Parent Handbook

- Vision and mission statement
- Program description, model, goals, and language allocation
- Student admission/placement process
- Dual Language Family Council
- Dual language family meetings and workshops
- Family nights and other annual events
- Volunteer opportunities
- Language of homework
- Family resources
- Frequently asked questions

FIGURE **3-13**
Dual Language Program Parent Handbook

Once these elements are in place, the Council selects projects and issues to undertake that can include a broad range of tasks and activities, such as facilitating parent support and workshops, family networking, as well as organizing events like cultural nights, award celebrations, and guest speakers. Family councils can also engage in advocacy efforts like reducing high-stakes testing or promoting program expansion and collaborating with community agencies for services and support. One such example of community collaboration is the Parent Mentor Program, a "nationally recognized parent engagement model that builds deep and lasting relationships between students, teachers, and parents" (Logan Square Neighborhood Association 2016). In this program, parent-mentors participate in leadership training and then are assigned to classrooms where they are mentored by the teacher as they work with students. After they have one hundred volunteer hours, they begin receiving a stipend (for more information, see www.lsna.net/Issues-and-programs/Schools-and-Youth/Parent-Mentor-Program.html).

Community Outreach

Community-based organizations such as the one mentioned above, as well as local businesses and government agencies, offer valuable resources for dual language programs and provide additional support for families. Community centers often offer ESL classes, continuing education, immigration assistance, and citizenship courses. Some community-based organizations help to establish "school-family advocacy partnerships to promote positive change in schools and districts. A school-family-community partnership approach offers the best opportunities for participation and engagement and also involves everyone in more meaningful ways" (Soltero 2011, 187). For middle and high schools that require students to complete service-learning hours, these can be done in community organizations where they can use their biliteracy and cross-cultural skills.

Increasingly, business leaders recognize the shared benefits that come from working collaboratively with schools. Local businesses can contribute funds, goods, or services to support dual language programs and also sponsor special events, awards, and fund-raising. For example, the Inter-American dual language school in Chicago is lucky enough to be blocks away from the historic Wrigley Field, home to the Chicago Cubs baseball team. Several years ago, they were visited by the entire baseball team and received a sizeable cash donation for their school. The then Chicago Cubs Manager Lou Piniella even spoke about his experiences growing up speaking Spanish and learning English when he entered first grade. For high school students, these school-business partnerships can also include college scholarships, work-study programs, school-to-career partnerships, internships, and job shadowing. These partnerships need to be carefully negotiated so that the school is not used for commercial purposes to sell products and services, or for marketing to students and their families. In addition, the National Association of Secondary School Principals suggests educators avoid partnering with businesses with controversial practices or political ties, and select companies that are socially responsible and promote academics and learning.

Supplementing the program with additional student supports in the L2 ensures they progress academically and acquire biliteracy. Some of these support systems can be integrated into the school curriculum, such as cross-age partnerships, global pen pals, sister dual language schools, and service learning. Others may be offered after school or in the summer, such as after-school culture and language clubs, tutoring sessions in the LOTE or ESL, or homework assistance. Global pen pals and dual language sister schools can be identified through social media and information that is readily available on the web. Networks can also provide opportunities for creating these transnational partnerships. Bettina, a teacher in the United States who attended an American K–12 bilingual school in Costa Rica and still had family in San José, connected with the principal to create a sister-school partnership that included pen pals, video conferences, and student collaborative multimedia projects. After eight years participating in this partnership, several teachers were able to visit each other's schools and are now planning to raise funds for the eighth-grade class to do a study exchange trip.

During the initial years, it is not uncommon for dual language programs to make adjustments in response to issues that arise during implementation. Because dual language education places additional demands on teachers and students, families play a critical role in supporting the teaching and learning that happens in school and continues at home. Families can be the most powerful advocates and promoters of dual language education, especially when their children succeed academically and become biliterate and cross-culturally competent.

Suggestions for Further Reading

Baker, Colin. 2014. *A Parents' and Teachers' Guide to Bilingualism*. Buffalo, NY: Multilingual Matters.

González, Norma, Luis Moll, and Cathy Amanti. 2005. *Funds of Knowledge: Theorizing Practices in Households, Communities, and Classrooms*. Mahwah, NJ: Lawrence Erlbaum Associates. ✳

CHAPTER

4

Bilingualism and Biliteracy

Strictly speaking, it would be difficult to find someone who thinks bilingualism is downright bad . . . to most people, having proficiency in two or more languages is considered a desirable attribute—one can reasonably argue that knowing two languages is better than knowing just one. Indeed, many people think that bilingualism is a sign of intellectual prowess and sophistication—those who have competence in several languages are often regarded with envy and admiration.

—Sarah Shin, *Bilingualism in School and Society*

The quote on the previous page seems to often apply to dominant language speakers but not so much for those who speak a nondominant language. In the United States, there is a predominant but puzzling view that bilinguals should become monolinguals and monolinguals should become bilinguals. That is, monolingual English speakers are encouraged to be bilingual, while those who speak a LOTE as their L1 are encouraged to become monolingual in English. Scalan and López (2015) suggest that "one way for school communities to cultivate language proficiency is by fostering cultures of bilingualism. This means acknowledging and embracing bilingualism as a norm and an ideal for all members of the school community" (101).

Bilingual education and second language acquisition might well be two of the most misunderstood education disciplines by those outside the field. Persistent misconceptions about teaching and learning in two languages continue to drive decisions about what role bilingualism should have in schools and how to educate ELs. A misinformed public perpetuates myths about bilingual education and L2 learning. These are the types of often-heard comments: children will be confused by being raised with two languages; the L1 is a crutch and should not be used; the fastest way to learn the L2 is through immersion; younger children acquire the L2 more easily and quickly than older students; parents should not speak to their children in the L1. Experts in the field show how each of these "myths" is refuted by facts and research findings (Crawford 2008; Espinosa 2013; McLaughlin 1992; Soltero 2011).

To complicate matters, general education teachers and school leaders tend to lack the necessary knowledge to make appropriate instructional decisions about ELs, often leading them to reject additive bilingual programs such as dual language education. Most teacher-preparation programs in the United States lack required university coursework in EL education. While teacher candidates are required to take courses in child development, classroom management, and special education, few teacher-preparation programs require coursework on the education of ELs. As a result, decisions based on misinformation about second language acquisition and bilingual development have long-term damaging consequences for students. The most harmful include low expectations for bilingual learners, unnecessary grade retention, student misclassification, increased rote learning, and premature removal from bilingual and dual language programs. The increasing number of linguistically diverse students in PK–12 classrooms, coupled with the current climate of accountability and high-stakes testing, require that all teachers and school leaders have adequate knowledge of culturally responsive and linguistically appropriate instruction and assessment practices (Goulah and Soltero 2015). A strong knowledge base about bilingualism and second language acquisition theories prepares dual language educators not only to respond to misconceptions with informed counterarguments, but also to advocate for the program. Dual language programs must make explicit the purpose for learning two languages, as well as the benefits of bilingualism and biliteracy, to students and families. These messages should be evident throughout the school and be ongoing for all stakeholders in both languages.

Bilingualism and Bilinguals

At first glance, bilingualism seems simple to define: the ability to use two languages. But bilinguals are much more nuanced and complex, accounting for different contexts in which they develop the two languages, their levels and types of proficiency in each language, and the dynamic nature of how their two languages change over time. The following section outlines the distinctions among bilinguals that need to be understood in the context of dual language education (see Figure 4-1).

Simultaneous bilinguals grow up using two languages from birth and therefore have two languages as their L1. Their bilingualism is developed in the same context (home), and they usually do not have an accent in either language. *Sequential bilinguals*, on the other hand, are school-age children or adults who learn the L2 after the L1, typically at school or after relocating to a place that uses the L2. *Circumstantial bilinguals* (also known as *folk bilinguals*) are usually from minority language groups that acquire the L2 in order to participate in the L2 community. They frequently

FIGURE **4-1**
Differences among
Bilinguals

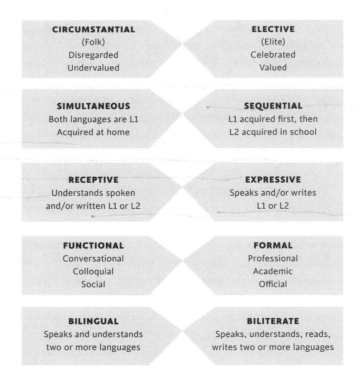

CIRCUMSTANTIAL
(Folk)
Disregarded
Undervalued

ELECTIVE
(Elite)
Celebrated
Valued

SIMULTANEOUS
Both languages are L1
Acquired at home

SEQUENTIAL
L1 acquired first, then
L2 acquired in school

RECEPTIVE
Understands spoken
and/or written L1 or L2

EXPRESSIVE
Speaks and/or writes
L1 or L2

FUNCTIONAL
Conversational
Colloquial
Social

FORMAL
Professional
Academic
Official

BILINGUAL
Speaks and understands
two or more languages

BILITERATE
Speaks, understands, reads,
writes two or more languages

have no schooling or literacy in the L1. Society tends to devalue their L1, resulting in a shift to L2 monolingualism within one or two generations. *Elective bilinguals* (also known as *elite bilinguals*), on the other hand, choose to become bilingual to enhance their social, educational, or employment opportunities and needs. These bilinguals tend to be biliterate, and are celebrated and valued by society. *Receptive bilinguals* can understand the less developed of the two languages but cannot speak, read, or write it well. They are typically individuals who come from a heritage language but have either never developed full proficiency or were at one time fluent but shifted to the L2. This often happens to children or grandchildren of immigrants or indigenous families, who are sometimes referred to as heritage language learners. Receptive bilinguals can also include those who learned a foreign language in school but no longer practice it. *Expressive bilinguals*, by contrast, can speak both languages but do not necessarily write either one unless they have had extended schooling in both languages. *Functional bilinguals* have conversational and social language skills in one or both languages, and use more colloquial expressions and code-switching than *formal bilinguals*, who have developed academic and/or professional skills in both languages. Finally, *biliterates* can read and write in two languages and typically have more formal, academic, and professional language skills than those who are only bilinguals.

Clearly bilinguals are not all the same. They come to be bilingual under a number of different circumstances, have different levels of proficiency in each language that can change over time, and use the two languages for different purposes and in different circumstances. Bilingualism itself involves complex cognitive and linguistic processes and interactions between the two languages. Because L2 acquisition and bilingual instruction are founded on so many theories that cannot be adequately covered in this book, I discuss a select few that are most relevant to dual language education. Research findings on the neurological and cognitive advantages of bilingualism are a precursor to understanding how bilinguals navigate the use of both languages. Jim Cummins, a leading scholar in the field of bilingual education, has contributed a number of theories that guide educators' understanding of bilingual development and L2 acquisition. These include the *threshold hypothesis*, the *academic vs. conversational distinction,* the *independence hypothesis*, and the *common underlying proficiency theory*.

Threshold Hypothesis

The *threshold hypothesis* proposes that learners need to reach a certain level of bilingualism to have positive effects on their cognitive and academic development (see Figure 4-2). The first threshold is the language proficiency level that students need to reach to avoid negative consequences of bilingualism, while the second threshold is needed to experience the full benefits of having developed two languages. *Limited bilinguals* are below the first threshold and do not have adequate age-appropriate

FIGURE **4-2**
The Threshold Hypothesis

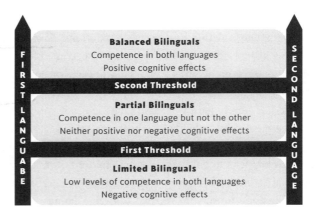

competence in either the L1 or L2. They have low L1 and L2 proficiency and may experience negative cognitive or academic consequences. Limited bilinguals include those who shifted to the L2 when very young, and typically receive weak L2 schooling and no L1 support. These students are not literate in the L1, may only have receptive L1 competencies, and speak a colloquial L1. *Partial bilinguals* have reached the first level and have age-appropriate competence in one language but not fully in the other. They do not experience either positive or negative consequences. These partial bilinguals include heritage language speakers with a fully developed L2 but limited L1 competence. For example, Chinese-speaking ELs who have acquired English and are no longer proficient in Chinese even though this was their L1 are considered partial bilinguals. *Balanced bilinguals* have reached the second threshold and have age-appropriate competence in both languages. This is the level that produces benefits and positive effects of bilingualism on students' cognitive and linguistic development (Cummins 2001).

According to Cummins, Mirza, and Stille (2012) ELs at the lower threshold "who are not supported in acquiring academic proficiency in the language of instruction, are likely to fall progressively further behind their peers in literacy development and overall school performance. Often there is little opportunity for these students to develop literacy skills in their L1, and thus they emerge from school without strongly developed literacy skills in either of their two languages. By contrast, when bilingual/ELL students are strongly supported in acquiring the language of instruction and encouraged to develop L1 literacy skills (either in school or home), an increasing amount of research suggests that they experience enhancement of cognitive and metalinguistic functioning" (29).

Having students reach the second threshold and become balanced bilinguals is the main goal of dual language education. The time it takes to develop academic L2 and the threshold hypothesis explain why dual language must be offered for at least six or eight years and why students need to stay for the duration of the program.

The threshold hypothesis provides a very powerful justification for additive bilingual education and for implementing dual language programs across the grade spans, elementary, middle, and high school.

stop

Academic vs. Conversational Distinction

One of the many common, but incorrect, views about learning an L2, especially for ELs, is that this process happens in a short time. Decades of research in the United States and abroad consistently show that developing academic L2 takes much longer than acquiring conversational L2 (Cummins 2008a). Researchers found that academic language (decontextualized and abstract, used in textbooks and schools) takes at least five to seven years to acquire compared to conversational language (supported by context cues, used in everyday social situations) that takes one to two years to develop. For example, words like *hence* and *thus* are academic and rarely used in every day conversation—instead, the equivalent high-frequency word *so* is used. Conversations between friends and family seldom involve words like *equilateral* or *arachnids*. These are academic words learned and used in school contexts (see Figure 4-3).

To support implementation and expansion of dual language education, it is particularly important for district and school leaders to understand *why* it takes so long to acquire academic L2. They should understand that conversational L2 takes less time to acquire than academic L2 because it is usually supported by context, is less dependent on prior knowledge, has fewer complex language structures, is made up of simple everyday words, and is driven by greater personal motivation. Academic L2, on the other hand, takes much longer to acquire because it has less context, more complex sentences, and more abstract, low-frequency, and content-based vocabulary (see Figure 4-4). Worth noting is that most native English speakers do

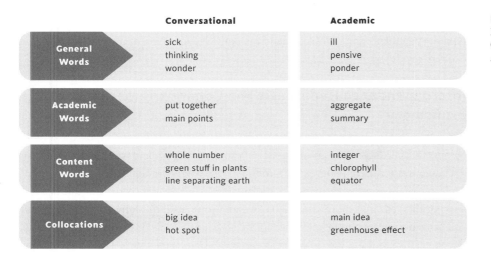

	Conversational	Academic
General Words	sick thinking wonder	ill pensive ponder
Academic Words	put together main points	aggregate summary
Content Words	whole number green stuff in plants line separating earth	integer chlorophyll equator
Collocations	big idea hot spot	main idea greenhouse effect

FIGURE **4-3**
Differences Between Conversational and Academic Words

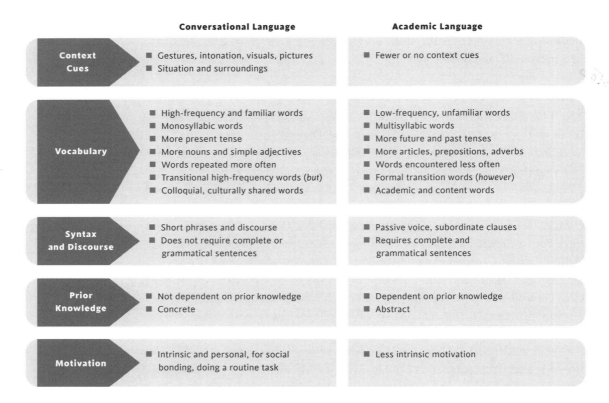

Conversational Language	Academic Language
Context Cues	
■ Gestures, intonation, visuals, pictures ■ Situation and surroundings	■ Fewer or no context cues
Vocabulary	
■ High-frequency and familiar words ■ Monosyllabic words ■ More present tense ■ More nouns and simple adjectives ■ Words repeated more often ■ Transitional high-frequency words (*but*) ■ Colloquial, culturally shared words	■ Low-frequency, unfamiliar words ■ Multisyllabic words ■ More future and past tenses ■ More articles, prepositions, adverbs ■ Words encountered less often ■ Formal transition words (*however*) ■ Academic and content words
Syntax and Discourse	
■ Short phrases and discourse ■ Does not require complete or grammatical sentences	■ Passive voice, subordinate clauses ■ Requires complete and grammatical sentences
Prior Knowledge	
■ Not dependent on prior knowledge ■ Concrete	■ Dependent on prior knowledge ■ Abstract
Motivation	
■ Intrinsic and personal, for social bonding, doing a routine task	■ Less intrinsic motivation

FIGURE **4-4**
Conversational and
Academic Language

not come to school with fully, or even partially, developed academic English. Native English-speaking students are unlikely to know words like *henceforth*, *aquifer*, and *hydrosphere*. Likewise, most native LOTE speakers do not come to school with highly developed academic LOTE. For example, Spanish-speaking students would not know words like *autótrofos* or *himenópteros*. Children and adolescents develop this type of vocabulary and complex academic language in school and over a long period of time, regardless of their L1.

Interdependence Hypothesis and Common Underlying Proficiency

The *interdependence hypothesis* asserts that L2 proficiency is dependent on the level of competence already achieved in the L1. In other words, the stronger the students' L1, the easier it is for them to develop a strong L2. Few would argue that learning new concepts and skills is more easily done in a language we fully command and understand, making this learning more comprehensive and long lasting. Many of those concepts and skills do not have to be relearned in the L2 but rather can be transferred to the L2. The concepts are the same, so only their new labels in the L2 need to be learned. The interdependence hypothesis is based on the notion that there is an underlying cognitive and academic proficiency common across all languages regardless of their distinct surface features (sounds, words, and grammar). This *common underlying proficiency* (CUP), also known as the *iceberg analogy*, drives thinking and is shared by the two languages, making academic concepts and skills in the L1 and L2 interdependent. The cognitive processes common across the two languages make transfer possible between the two and help to develop metabilingual awareness (see Figure 4-5).

In the iceberg analogy, observable linguistic features like words, sounds, and grammar are above the surface and are different between the two languages. For example, in English the adjective goes before the noun (*big house*) but in Spanish it is the opposite (*casa grande*); the sound *th* in *thing* does not exist in many LOTEs, and the Spanish double *rr* sound does not exist in English. Below the surface, the two languages function together as one source of thinking that includes semantics (meaning) and pragmatics (appropriate language use according to context). To make this more concrete, consider the difference and similarities between driving in the United Kingdom and the United States. On the surface, they are different because one is done on the left and the other on the right side of the road. However, the fundamental skills involved in driving remain the same. Knowing how to drive represents the underlying common proficiency, while the logistic differences of driving on the right- or left-hand side of the road represent the distinct surface features.

Cognitive Advantages of Bilingualism

The belief that bilingualism and learning in two languages cause confusion and cognitive problems is another common myth. Families are often advised by teachers, counselors, and sometimes medical professionals, to avoid raising their children

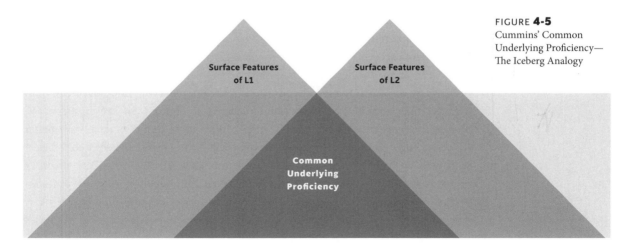

FIGURE **4-5**
Cummins' Common Underlying Proficiency— The Iceberg Analogy

bilingually because this will lead to cognitive handicaps. The association between "mental retardation" and bilingualism in the United States has a sad place in history dating to the early 1900s and was particularly damaging for Mexican heritage students. According to Flores (2005), children were "intentionally segregated from their Anglo counterparts because their Spanish language was assumed to retard their achievement in English language instruction" (76). She adds that "the myth of 'mental retardation' because of 'language difficulty' among Spanish speaking children" (76) led researchers, who administered cognitive tests in English to non-English-speaking students, to conclude that these difficulties were caused by a "bilingual problem." By the 1950s, bilingualism became a "language handicap" and was considered one of the official causes of "retardation." Extensive research findings refute these assumptions and affirm that bilingualism has no negative consequences for students' academic or linguistic development.

According to psycholinguists and neuroscience researchers, bilinguals experience significant cognitive advantages because they manage two languages at all times. Bilingualism is a kind of mental workout that fine-tunes thinking, enhances metalinguistic awareness, and expands understanding of language structures critical for literacy. In simple terms, *metalinguistic awareness* is the ability to think and talk about language. This conscious awareness helps students understand and manipulate language. Students who have well-developed metalinguistic awareness engage the deep structure of language (semantics and pragmatics). They know what register to use, when and with whom to use it, what words are appropriate according to context, how to put words and sentences together to change meaning, and how to interpret nuances in language (like humor, sarcasm, or idiomatic expressions). Students have better awareness of sounds, syllables, words, phrases, and sentences and know how to manipulate them to change meaning. Bilinguals have an enhanced awareness of these types of language processes because they constantly interact with the world through two languages.

An influential study conducted by Peal and Lambert (1962) found that bilingual students scored higher than their monolingual peers in IQ tests that assessed their abilities to distinguish metalinguistic features and ignore distractions when performing a task. In the last decade, findings from a growing body of research affirm the many cognitive benefits of bilingualism (see Figure 4-6). The most compelling conclusions are that bilinguals, when compared to monolinguals, have better executive functioning cognitive processing, attention control, and also cope better with neurological diseases. Bialystok, Craik, and Luk (2012) studied the effects of bilingualism on cognitive functions and found that bilinguals, compared to monolinguals, perceive differences and hold attention longer because they have a more efficient and developed executive control. Their findings suggest that bilinguals

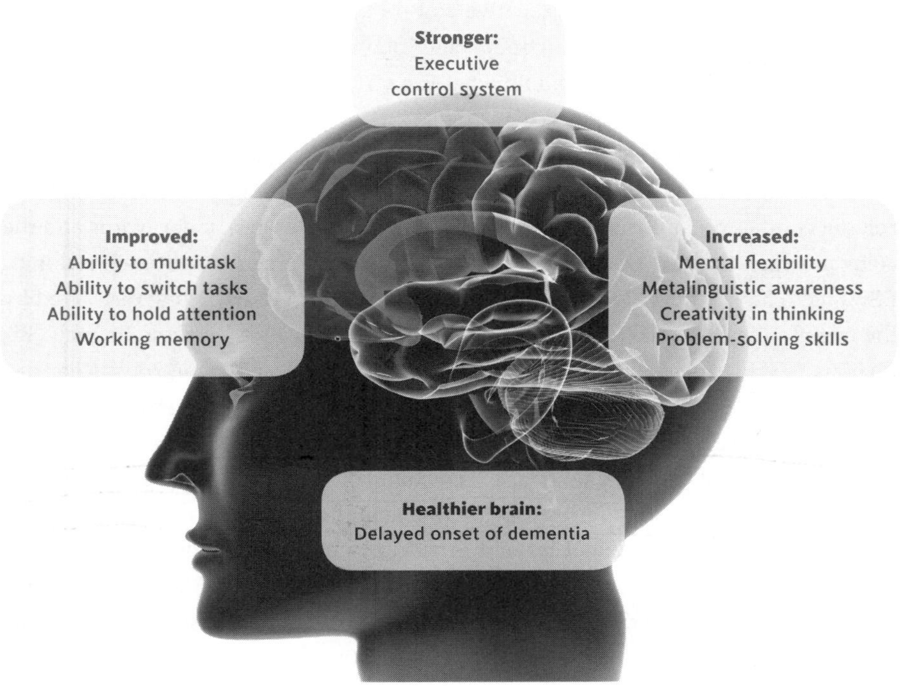

FIGURE **4-6**
Cognitive Advantages of
Bilingualism

Stronger:
Executive
control system

Improved:
Ability to multitask
Ability to switch tasks
Ability to hold attention
Working memory

Increased:
Mental flexibility
Metalinguistic awareness
Creativity in thinking
Problem-solving skills

Healthier brain:
Delayed onset of dementia

perform better on cognitive tasks using different brain networks that lead to improved working memory, more effective multitasking, and increased inhibition of irrelevant information. They concluded that "lifelong experience in managing attention in two languages reorganizes specific brain networks, creating a more effective basis for executive control and sustaining better cognitive performance throughout the lifespan" (241).

The executive control system, the part of the brain responsible for higher-order thinking and problem-solving, is more developed in bilinguals than in monolinguals. Bialystok (2011) contends that the constant exercising of the executive control system in the bilingual brain leads to a greater number of neurological connections and strengthens the brain. A stronger executive control system results in neurological advantages in perception, attention, selection of relevant information, resolving conflicting information, and protection from cognitive diseases. These types of structural changes in the bilingual brain help to delay the onset of Alzheimer's among bilinguals. For bilinguals, the functioning of the brain is changed by the continual demands to make choices about which language to use, restructuring brain functions and resulting in a healthier and more flexible brain (Bak et al. 2014).

Three components of the executive control system are more developed in bilinguals: multitasking, working memory, and inhibition/selection. Working memory includes auditory memory (recalling what is heard) and visual-perception memory (recalling what is seen). Multitasking is the ability to cognitively engage in many activities at the same time. *Inhibition* refers to the ability to selectively pay attention to some tasks and ignore others. Bilinguals perform better on tasks that require resolving conflicting information. For example, in the Stroop test, color words and the color in which they are written do not match (the word green is written in red ink). Bilinguals can say the color in which it is written (red) without being distracted by the meaning of the word (green) faster and more accurately than monolinguals. Bilinguals perform better on these tasks because their executive control system can more easily suppress reading the word and focus on the color of the text.

For bilinguals, their two languages are activated at all times, even if the context requires the use of only one language. This *joint activation* is a constant distraction that forces bilinguals to suppress one language and activate the other, a cognitive exercise of the brain that is not present in monolinguals. Bilinguals constantly have to analyze and select the correct language from competing options. For example, Spanish-English bilinguals subconsciously have to make decisions on communicating formality in English vs. Spanish (Spanish has two forms for formal/informal—*tú/usted*—but English does not); Chinese-English bilinguals have to determine communicating past tense in English vs. Chinese (English has past tense but Chinese does not). Bialystok, Craik, and Luk (2012) argue that "although joint activation creates a risk for language interference and language errors, these rarely occur, indicating that the selection of the target language occurs with great accuracy" (241). Whether bilinguals are speaking to monolinguals or bilinguals determines what aspect of their two languages are activated. That is, when speaking to monolinguals, bilinguals activate one language and suppress the other, but when speaking to other bilinguals, they activate both languages. Code-switching is an example of the cognitive flexibility and control of task-switching between the two languages.

Code-Switching

Stable code-switching is a rule-governed mechanism used by most bilinguals to fill linguistic gaps, place emphasis in speech, create cultural bonding with other speakers of the two languages, and establish shared cultural identity (Grosjean 2010). To capitalize on students' metabilingual awareness and expand their bilingual skills, teachers must understand how the two languages intersect and influence each other. This extended discussion on code-switching provides examples of cross-linguistic connections, metalinguistic strategies, and other instructional approaches that support bilingual and biliterate development. While the majority of the cross-linguistic examples provided here are in Spanish-English, many can be applied to other languages.

The following two statements are matter-of-fact realities: (1) Dual language teachers and students use two languages for classroom communication and instructional interaction; (2) Code-switching is a natural and normal linguistic behavior of bilinguals. Based on these two premises, it is essential to understand what code-switching is and when, how, and by whom it should be used in the classroom. Although code-switching is common among bilinguals, it is also often misunderstood and frowned on by educators, parents, and even bilinguals themselves (Shin 2013). Teachers and families frequently view code-switching as random mixing of two languages due to interference or confusion. Some go as far as to link code-switching with low intelligence and poor education. But extensive research shows code-switching is not detrimental to the acquisition of the L2, suggesting that classroom code-switching "is a teaching/learning aid that can be used to meet a wide range classroom needs" (Kamwangamalu 2010, 128).

Another common view is that code-switchers are only those who come from low-income backgrounds with limited education. But this is not the case. For example, respected Latin American newspapers like the *Financial Times* in Spanish, *El Financiero*, which is read by educated middle-class Spanish speakers, frequently uses the loan word *defoltear*. Spanish does not have a single word for *default*, so the meaning in Spanish has to be conveyed in a long sentence: *Las deudas no pueden ser pagadas con los acreedores, que resulta en un acuerdo entre el deudor y los acreedores bajo supervisión judicial sobre el modo en que se pagará.* It makes sense to borrow the word from English and convert it to Spanish to express the concept in a more concise way. Social media also has many interesting examples of borrowing from English. Spanish speakers, for example, use words like *el face* for Facebook, *tuiteando* for tweeting, and *chatear* for online chatting. These types of borrowed words from English social media are also evident in many other LOTEs.

Mixing of the two languages happens more frequently within the sentence (intersentential) but also happens across sentences (intrasentential) and includes transferring, borrowing, loan words, derivational blends, and calques. Calques are particularly interesting, because they are literal translations of words or phrases from another language that have a different meaning. For example, *groserías* in Spanish means rude remarks, but when it is translated literally from the word *groceries* it becomes a calque, a word that is not used in standard Spanish to refer to food produce (*comida*) (see Figure 4-7).

Different registers call for different language use. Much like general education students who need to understand differences between everyday colloquial English and academic Standard English, and know when and with whom to use each,

FIGURE **4-7**
Types of Code-Switching

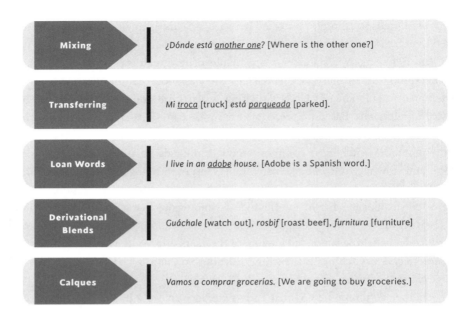

Mixing	¿Dónde está *another one*? [Where is the other one?]
Transferring	Mi *troca* [truck] está *parqueada* [parked].
Loan Words	I live in an *adobe* house. [Adobe is a Spanish word.]
Derivational Blends	Guáchale [watch out], rosbif [roast beef], furnitura [furniture]
Calques	Vamos a comprar grocerías. [We are going to buy groceries.]

students in dual language programs must also develop and know when to use academic LOTE and the differences between standard and colloquial LOTE. Spanish is more challenging because of the many regional differences in vocabulary and idiomatic expressions across the twenty-plus countries and territories in which Spanish is the majority language. Adding to this complexity are the everyday *Spanglish* colloquialisms spoken by Latino communities in the United States. Dual language students should study and discuss this type of hybrid language that arises when two or more languages coexist. For example, Figure 4-8 shows a fourth-grade dual language

FIGURE **4-8**
Word Wall with Two
Varieties of Spanish

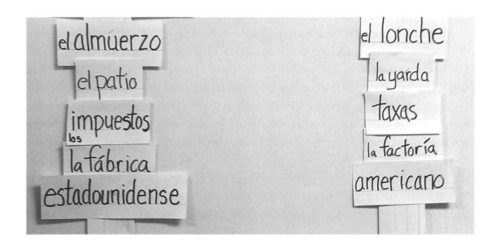

classroom word wall with differences between two varieties of Spanish. A particularly challenging issue is deciding what to call these two registers. Some refer to one as the *language of school* and the other as *the language of home*. But this may send a negative message that the language of home is less valued than that of school, rather than just make the distinction between the two. Faced with this challenge, a dual language teacher decided to call one *Spanish of Latin America and Spain* and the other *Spanish of the United States*.

Julia Alvarez, Walter Dean Meyers, Gary Soto, Sandra Cisneros, and Junot Díaz are examples of authors who use code-switching as a literary device to add flavor, play with languages, and reflect group membership and cultural identity (Chappell and Faltis 2006; Martin 2005). Puerto Rican author Giannina Braschi published *Yo-Yo Boing!*, an all-Spanglish novel that, on Amazon, lists Spanglish as the language of the book. Code-switching is also frequently used in music like Arabic-French *rai* or Spanglish *reggaetton*. The Korenglish song *Gangnam Style* by Korean pop star Psy is almost entirely in Korean but has English in the title and throughout the song. Shakira, a Colombian singer-songwriter, and Pitbull, a Cuban American rapper, are both known for using Spanish-English code-switching in many of their songs. This type of creative and authentic code-switching can be used by students to analyze and discuss linguistic and cultural features, and to create their own code-switched books, raps, poetry, or songs. Shin (2013) refers to the creation of these sorts of new languages and art forms as "transcultural flow" that arises from increasing contact between languages across the world.

While code-switching is common in many border communities and multilingual regions of the world, the United States is unique because of its large population of Spanish-English bilinguals. According to a 2015 report from the Instituto Cervantes, the United States now has more Spanish speakers (fifty-two million) than Spain (forty-seven million) (Fernández Vítores 2015). Across the globe, Spanish which is spoken in 31 countries, is the second most spoken language—after Chinese—with 427 million L1 speakers, while English is third, with 339 million L1 speakers (Ethnologue 2016). Reflecting this widespread use of Spanish in the United States, the *Academia Norteamericana de la Lengua Española* (North American Academy of the Spanish Language) was established in 1973 to support and promote the use of Spanish in the United States. Among other information, they offer lists of *estadounidismo* (Spanish words from the United States) such as *rentar, bagel, pretzel*, and *van*. Some Spanglish words, like *parquear* and *aparcar* (borrowed from *parking, estacionar* in standard Spanish) are so common that they have been accepted into the Real Academia Española, an institution in Spain that monitors correct Spanish usage. Spanglish in the United States is increasingly used in advertisements, television, radio, and print. For the dual language classroom, real-life examples can be used to explore grammar and vocabulary features of each language and how they interact in print. For example, teachers might model writing code-switched greeting cards and use them as a springboard for students to create their own greeting cards (see Figure 4-9). As Shin (2013) points out, "Bilingualism sells. Throughout the world, marketers promote products and services through bilingual advertisements to target customers who are bilingual" (37). Products such as Spanglish greeting cards sell in the United States because of the critical mass of Spanish-English bilinguals needed to market them. For other LOTE speakers in the United States such as Chinese, Arabic, and Vietnamese communities, code-switching appears in similar hybrid cultural-linguistic adaptations that can be used as teaching tools in the classroom.

In dual language programs, code-switching is an aspect of language acquisition that has to be understood in the context of natural bilingual development. While teachers should avoid code-switching, they should encourage bilingual students who are at the beginner and intermediate levels to use their two languages to fill in gaps or for clarification. This is illustrated in Figure 4-10.

The purpose for providing this extended discussion on code-switching is to situate it within the instructional scope of the dual language classroom. That is, examples of student and societal code-switching can be used as a tool to expand students' metabilingual awareness, as a bridge to understand different registers, and to engage in creative cross-cultural language activities. It is important to note that, while code-switching and colloquial hybrids of two languages are a natural part of becoming and being bilingual, students need to develop the standard language

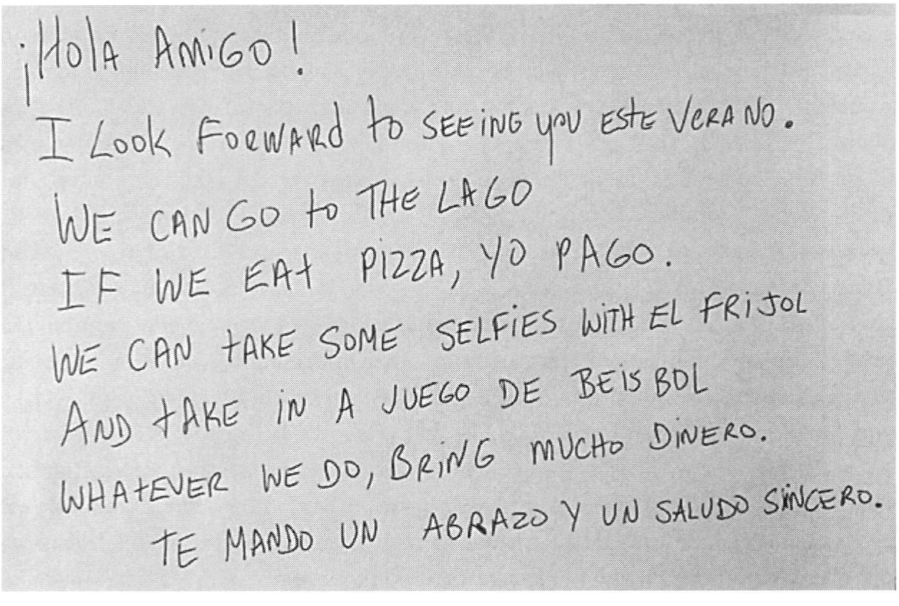

FIGURE 4-9
Spanglish Greeting Card

¡Hola Amigo!
I look forward to seeing you este verano.
We can go to the lago
If we eat pizza, yo pago.
We can take some selfies with el frijol
And take in a juego de beisbol
Whatever we do, bring mucho dinero.
Te mando un abrazo y un saludo sincero.

FIGURE **4-10**
Code-Switching in a Dual
Language Kindergarten

> **An English-dominant African American student requesting information and clarification from the Spanish dual language team-teacher:**
>
> Student A: Maestra, where do I put the libro? [*Teacher, where do I put the book?*]
> Teacher: Ponlo allá, en la canasta. [*Put it over there, in the basket.*]
> Student A: Canasta? What's that? [*Basket? What's that?*]
> Teacher: Si, aquí en la canasta. [*Yes, here in the basket.*]
> Student A: Oh, the basket . . . canasta . . . OK. [*Oh, the basket . . . the basket . . . OK.*]
> Student B: What did she say?
> Student A: To put it in the basket . . . canasta. [*To put it in the basket . . . basket.*]

variety and vocabulary of each language and know how and when to use or not to use code-switching.

Metabilingual Awareness and Cross-Linguistic Strategies

Metabilingual awareness allows students to understand how their two languages interact and influence each other. L2 errors, for instance, are often influenced by the L1. For example, Spanish-speaking ELs find articles difficult. They might say, "Maria is looking for *one* book to read" (*Maria esta buscando* un *libro para leer*) because in Spanish there is no distinction between the indefinite article (*un, uno, una*) and the number one (*uno*). For Chinese-speaking ELs, the cross-linguistic difficulties appear in verb tenses and plurals. They may say, "Xian *go* to many *school* in Beijing when he young." Russian and other Slavic languages do not have articles (*the, a, an*)—instead, they have one of three gender articles: male, female, and neutral. So a Russian EL might say, "Book is good but *she* is too long." Making these differences and similarities explicit in teaching and learning facilitates transfer from one language to the other and helps students understand the sources of their errors.

Cross-linguistic strategies allow students to compare and contrast words, grammar, sounds, and idiomatic expressions between the two languages. This type of teaching for transfer happens in planned lessons and also throughout the day as *teachable moments* that come up more spontaneously. Informal connections happen when language similarities and differences occur in the course of a classroom discussions, lessons, or while reading and writing. Some schools implement *bridging lessons* (Beeman and Urow 2012) that take place during designated teaching-for-transfer instruction in the form of "bridging" through cognate word walls and bridging charts (see Figure 4-11). Beyond this specific time, teachers at all grade levels should engage students in metabilingual strategies, cross-linguistic connections, and teaching for transfer throughout the day.

The most common cross-linguistic connections are cognates, words in two languages with similar spelling, pronunciation, and meaning. Languages with cognates

FIGURE **4-11**
Teaching-for-Transfer
Cognate Chart

in English have a significant number of words with Latin and Greek roots, including Romance languages (Spanish, French, Portuguese, Italian, and Romanian) and also German, Dutch, and Greek. Spanish and English share many cognates, including high-frequency words like *doctor-doctor* and more academic abstract low-frequency words like *condensation-condensación*. Low-frequency cognates can be especially helpful as scaffolds for students when learning L2 content. Worth noting is that students do not generally come to school knowing these types of academic and content words in English or the LOTE. Once students learn the new concept and word associated with it, then the cognate transfer happens more effectively. Cognate strategies include cognate word banks, word sorts, and word walls, underlining or highlighting cognates, and activities like cognate detective or false-cognate detective, where students find these while reading or writing a text or when they hear or say them (see Figure 4-12).

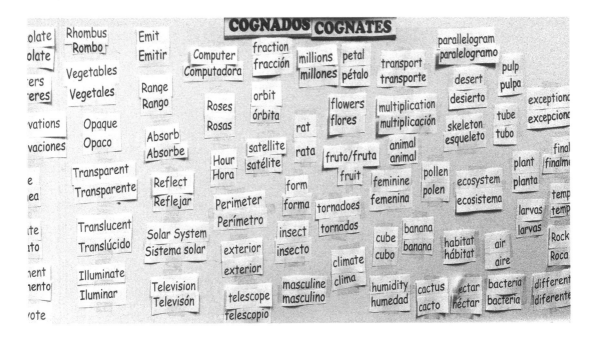

FIGURE **4-12**
Cognate Word Wall

Patterns in prefixes and suffixes across two languages can be used to make further cross-linguistic connection. For example, in English every word that ends in –*ly* (as in *strategically*) ends in –*mente* (as in *estrategicamente*) in Spanish. The most useful aspect is that many academic low-frequency words in English are common everyday high-frequency words in Spanish, such as *obscure* in English and the common everyday word *oscuro* in Spanish (see Figure 4-13).

FIGURE **4-13**
Types of Spanish-English Cognates

Cognates		False Cognate	
error	error	once	once
historia	history	sobre	sober
atlas	atlas	fábrica	fabric

High-Frequency in Both		Low-Frequency in Both	
color	color	península	peninsula
idea	idea	trapezóide	trapezoid
hospital	hospital	hábitat	habitat

Prefixes		Suffixes	
infraestructura	infrastructure	finalmente	finally
interactuar	interact	acción	action
rehacer	redo	considerable	considerable
posponer	postpone	lunático	lunatic
antibiótico	antibiotic	responsabilidad	responsibility

High-Frequency in Spanish	Low-Frequency in English
enfermo	infirm
edificio	edifice
pálido	pallid
culpable	culpable

Other differences and similarities between the two languages for students to explore include word order, plurals, articles and gender articles, and verb tenses. For example, during a lesson about land forms, the teacher can write *geographic characteristics* and *características geográficas* on the board and ask students to analyze the differences between the two: the word order is reversed, accent in one language but not the other, *ph-f* and *ch-c* spelling and sound; and the similarities between the two, cognates and the prefix *geo*. In addition to grammar and vocabulary cross-linguistic analysis, students can also compare and contrast idiomatic expression, literal vs. figurative language, and how/why literal translations often do not convey the intended meaning. For example, idioms do not translate well from one language to another, and often become humorous nonsense when translated.

Spanish idiom:	Como quitarle un pelo a un gato.
Literal translation:	Like pulling a hair off a cat.
Equivalent English idiom:	Like a drop in the bucket.
Spanish idiom:	Camarón que se duerme, se lo lleva la corriente.
Literal translation:	The shrimp that falls asleep is carried away by the current.
Equivalent English idiom:	You snooze, you lose.
Spanish idiom:	De tal palo, tal astilla.
Literal translation:	From this stick, this splinter.
Equivalent English idiom:	A chip off the old block.

Translanguaging

Translanguaging, a term first used by Cen Williams in 1994, was conceptualized as a pedagogical tool that uses two languages for instruction, where receptive language (reading and listening) may be in one language and expressive language (speaking and writing) may be in the other. For example, in a dual language Chinese-English program, students hear and read about the Civil War in English and then create and present a digital slideshow about it in Chinese. Later, the students read about the Battle of Gettysburg in Chinese and write a report about it in English. Baker (2011) defines translanguaging as "the process of making meaning, shaping experiences, gaining understanding and knowledge through the use of two languages" (288). More recently, the concept of translanguaging was expanded by García (2009) to describe the everyday flexible language practices of bilinguals who constantly and interchangeably use their two languages to interact and make sense of the world. For García, translanguaging is both the discourse practices of bilinguals and a pedagogical tool that taps into students' bilingual knowledge and resources to learn academic language and content. These discourse practices include the nonstandard varieties and code-mixing that result when two languages come into contact over time, as well as cross-linguistic instructional approaches discussed earlier in this chapter. Translanguaging does not follow rigid boundaries for each language in the classroom, so students are free to choose what language to use. García clarifies that translanguaging must be used strategically as a teaching strategy and learning tool.

While the concepts embedded in translanguaging are relevant to dual language education, the idea of fluid language boundaries can be incompatible with its programmatic foundations. In the context of dual language, the separation of the two languages for instruction is necessary for the reasons outlined in Chapters 2 and 3, so the premise to eliminate language allocation and formal separation of the two languages would not be suitable. However, many other aspects of students' translanguaging are valuable for dual language teachers as instructional tools, especially cross-linguistic instructional practices and the recognition and value of the language hybridity practices of bilinguals.

Biliteracy

The previous discussions on how the two languages of emergent bilinguals interact in cognitive processes, how bilingual brains function and benefit from handling two languages, the intersection of the two languages in code-switching, and the use of cross-linguistic connections to expand students' metabilingual awareness provide the basis for formulating sound biliteracy practices. Hornberger's (2004) *continua of biliteracy* speaks to the complexities in developing reading and writing in two languages, including decisions on how to approach standard vs. nonstandard varieties of the LOTE. She argues that teachers should consider "code-switching and language mixing practices, as learners draw on all the available communicative resources in their developing biliteracy" and adds, "language mixing very often enables educators to contextualize and communicate academic content to multilingual learners" (162).

Many features of literacy are universal and transfer between the L1 and L2. For example, narrative text elements are universal across written languages. Stories in all languages have a beginning, middle, and end, as well as characters, plot, setting, problem, and solution. Expository texts in written languages all have similar structures such as tables of contents, headings and subheadings, indexes, and captions. Other universal literacy features include strategies to derive meaning from text like inferencing, predicting, summarizing, and questioning. All these universal aspects of literacy only need to be learned once and can then be transferred to the L2. Learning the fundamentals of reading and writing only happens once. Some aspects of language and literacy do not transfer, either because they do not exist in one of the languages or because they have culturally based meanings. Idiomatic expressions are especially difficult for language learners because they require shared cultural knowledge.

[handwritten margin note:] Literacy strategies). - inferencing. - predicting - summarizing - questioning.

Developing literacy in the L2 does not involve starting from zero again. Rather, once students develop an understanding of print concepts, alphabetic principle, text structures, and how to use cues to create meaning from text in one language, they transfer this knowledge to the process of reading and writing in the other language (August and Shanahan 2010; Hopewell and Escamilla 2014). This transfer is explained in the *common underlying proficiency* and *interdependence hypothesis* discussed earlier in the chapter. When students read in their L2, they apply knowledge they have about literacy in the L1 to reading and writing in the L2, like making inferences and predictions to make sense of the text.

Strong literacy development in the L1 facilitates overall academic achievement and proficiency in the L2, especially for ELs (Krashen and McField 2005; Goldenberg and Coleman 2010; Rolstad, Mahoney, and Glass 2005; Slavin and Cheung 2003). Developing strong literacy skills often depends on the types of instructional approaches, materials, and assessments used. Focusing on reading mechanics alone, at the expense of language development, falls short in supporting students' overall academic achievement (Callahan 2006). Dual language students will not develop the comprehension or vocabulary necessary to do well academically in the L2 if the emphasis is only on isolated word recognition, spelling, and decoding skills. Students need to acquire extensive content-based and academic vocabulary as well as strategies for comprehending and analyzing demanding expository text in meaningful ways (Genesee et al. 2006).

Language of Emergent Literacy

Whether to teach emergent literacy sequentially (in the L1 or the LOTE first) or simultaneously (both at the same time) continues to be debated. The L1-L2 transfer view of biliteracy would support emergent literacy development in the L1 "so that cognitive skills and strategies needed for reading can be fully developed . . . these literacy skills and strategies transfer easily and readily to the second language" (Baker 2011, 323). Others point out that learning to read and write in both languages at the same time has no detrimental effects. Studies conducted in dual language programs reveal that native English speakers can successfully learn to read and write in their L2 first, before they have developed literacy in their L1 (Thomas and Collier 2012). Research in Canada and the United States also shows that teaching literacy through the L2 to majority language students in dual language programs does not interfere with their acquisition of literacy in their L1 or the development of the two languages, even for low-income African American students in French immersion programs (Thomas and Collier 2012).

Deciding on simultaneous vs. sequential emergent (PK–1) literacy instruction depends on a number of factors. Teaching young children to read and write in two languages at the same time can create challenges, especially in partial immersion programs. A significant amount of time is already dedicated in the early grades to language and literacy development in one language. To add literacy in another language may dilute literacy instruction of both languages due to time constraints, overload of similar and divergent literacy concepts in each language, and less time for content area learning. Students who do not have a solid oral language in their L1 and are taught to read in two languages at the same time may not fully internalize the letter-sound code well enough in either language. While learning literacy in two languages simultaneously occurs successfully in some cases, my recommendation is to follow a sequential order of emergent literacy instruction, especially for ELs who would benefit from first developing a strong literacy and language base in their L1 and later in their L2.

In partial immersion, students develop emergent literacy either in their L1 (English for English-dominant students and LOTE for ELs) or in both languages simultaneously. In 90-10 total immersion models, all students typically develop emergent literacy in the LOTE, while in 80-20 models emergent literacy can be either in the LOTE for all students or in both languages simultaneously. For example, in a Navajo-English total immersion program, Navajo- and English-dominant students all learn to read and write in Navajo first. Gradually, throughout the primary grades, English literacy instruction is introduced, and eventually all students become biliterate. Research points to the many benefits for ELs who learn to read and write in their L1 first. However, for native English speakers in two-way programs, other factors need to be considered. In deciding on the language of emergent literacy instruction, programs must carefully consider students' language and literacy experiences, background knowledge of literacy and linguistic concepts, family literacy support, and mobility. English-dominant students who lack adequate skills in their L1 and have fewer literacy-related experiences at home may be better off developing emergent literacy in their L1. For English-dominant students who enter school with strong L1 and literacy foundations, emergent literacy instruction can be in the LOTE. On the other hand, for English-dominant students with weak L1 and literacy foundations, emergent literacy should be in English. Programs should review and analyze how the language of emergent literacy instruction model is working and monitor how students are performing academically in third grade and above. From this data, schools are able to determine if the model of literacy instruction should continue or be changed.

In some schools where students receive simultaneous literacy instruction in PK–1, ELs are taught English phonics with instructional curriculum designed for English-speaking students. This can be quite detrimental, especially for ELs at the beginning language proficiency levels, because they do not yet have enough vocabulary or oral language in English. The sounds that beginner ELs learn cannot be attached to any meaning because they have not yet developed enough vocabulary. Rather than giving direct instruction on phonics, ELs in PK–1 should be exposed to English phonemic awareness and phonics through more contextualized and meaningful approaches, like shared reading and shared writing, rhymes and songs, word plays, and use of predictable and pattern-language books. In fourth grade and above, language arts should be in both languages, except for students who enroll after second grade and may still be at a beginner L2 level (this would apply to ELs).

Differentiating the Language of Classroom Print

The print in the classroom must reflect the language distribution of the grade level. For example, if the language distribution in PK–1 is 80-20, then about eighty percent of the print should be in the LOTE and about twenty percent in English. If in third grade it is 60-40, then about sixty percent of the print should be in the LOTE and forty percent in English. Color-coding classroom print and books, especially in the early grades, provides a scaffold for students to know if they have to apply English or LOTE phonics when trying to decode classroom print and books. For example, when students who are developing early literacy in the primary grades come across a word like *dime*, it would help them to know if they have to apply English phonics (*dime* is a ten-cent coin) or Spanish syllables (*dime* is *tell me*). Similarly, a word like *pie* when read in English is a dessert but when read in Spanish is a foot. Color-coding each language should be uniform across grade levels to ensure consistency for students, so dual language teachers should agree on two colors and use them consistently. Books in the early grades (PK–3) can also be color-coded with red and blue stickers for each language. Color-coding of the two languages provides an additional scaffold for students but also helps teachers to visually represent the amount of print in the two languages that corresponds to the language allocation.

Suggestions for Further Reading

Escamilla, Kathy, Susan Hopewell, and Sandra Butvilofsky. 2013. *Biliteracy from the Start: Literacy Squared in Action.* Philadelphia: Caslon Publishing.

Rodríguez, Diane, Angela Carrasquillo, and Kung Soon Lee. 2014. *The Bilingual Advantage: Promoting Academic Development, Biliteracy, and Native Language in the Classroom.* New York: Teachers College Press. ✳

Dual Language Instruction and Assessment Practices

Task-based and content-based approaches maintain that students benefit from receiving interrelated target language input by both listening and reading on multiple occasions as well as having multiple opportunities to express similar ideas in the target language. All these approaches support the idea that language classes should include a mix of language skills and coordinated set of learning activities.

—Elaine K. Horwitz, *Becoming A Language Teacher*

earning works best when students are engaged in thinking, problem solving, connecting to their prior knowledge, and making sense of ideas and concepts in collaboration with others. For dual language classrooms, constructivist and student-centered instruction is especially important because transmission-oriented approaches, such as memorization of isolated skills and rote learning, prevent bilingual learners from being fully engaged with new content in their L2. Constructivist approaches are based on Vygotsky's (1978) theories that the acquisition of knowledge and development of cognition are socially constructed and shared processes. These cognitive processes happen collaboratively through language in social interactions. Engaging students in using their two languages for meaningful academic and sociocultural purposes results in higher levels of achievement (Collier and Thomas 2012; de Jong 2004; Genesee et al. 2006).

Assessment practices that align with the developmental nature of becoming bilingual and biliterate must also be carefully considered. Baker (2011) cautions that "the testing of bilinguals has developed from the practices of testing monolinguals. Bilinguals are not the simple sum of two monolinguals but are a unique combination and integration of languages" (355). Having a strategic and comprehensive system to measure, monitor, and collect data on students' academic, bilingual, and biliterate progress better positions schools to demonstrate that their dual language program produces positive learning outcomes.

Instructional Approaches for Second Language Development

Harper and de Jong (2009) argue against the popular notion that teaching L2 learners is only "a matter of applying 'just good teaching' practices developed for a diverse group of native English speakers" (102). While many teaching strategies are indeed effective with all students, including ELs, teachers should understand that learning in an L2 requires specialized instructional approaches and "pedagogical tools" that take into account students' language proficiency levels as well as L2 acquisition processes. The use of bilingual and L2 strategies provide the needed temporary supports for academic and language development as students become fully biliterate and independent learners. Practices such as cooperative learning, thematic approach, and instructional conversations are also particularly effective for students learning in two languages. These types of approaches encourage active participation in the learning process while interacting in meaningful and purposeful communication in both languages.

Bilingual Instructional Strategies

Several strategies that are specially designed for L2 instruction can facilitate students' scaffolded engagement with language and content. These strategies include *Preview-Review*, *Total Physical Response*, and *Language Experience Approach*.

Preview-Review is a bilingual strategy that provides comprehensible input through a brief preview of the lesson in the L1 before the content is presented in the L2 and is then followed by a review in the L1 (see Figure 5-1). The teacher first *previews* the lesson in the L1 for four to five minutes, through a variety of strategies like summaries of key concepts and vocabulary, activation of prior knowledge, anticipatory guides or KWL charts, chapter walks or picture walks, or short video. This is followed by the *view*, a thirty- to forty-minute lesson in the L2 that includes differentiation and modifications for different language proficiency levels. The lesson concludes with a four- to five-minute *review* in the L1 that may include summarizing key ideas and vocabulary, reflecting on what was just learned, or completing the anticipation guide or KWL chart. While the Preview-Review strategy uses the two languages within a lesson, each language is used in a deliberate way during very specific times. Therefore, this is not considered code-switching or translation. Also, it is worth noting that this strategy should not be used for every lesson, but rather as a scaffold while introducing new material or concepts that are especially challenging.

Total Physical Response (TPR) relies on teacher and student physical movements to teach and learn vocabulary and concepts in the L2. This strategy provides context-embedded comprehensible language and opportunities to engage in kinesthetic learning. In TPR, students listen and physically respond to oral commands that are modeled by the teacher. At first, students listen and respond to simple commands given by the teacher, such as "Touch your elbow," or "Stand up." As students advance in their L2, the commands become more cognitively and linguistically demanding—for example, "Stand behind a classmate who is taller than you." In order to respond to this command, students must know the concepts of *taller* and *behind*. Also, literal and figurative language can be better understood through TPR. For example, students can follow commands to reenact figurative and literal meanings of

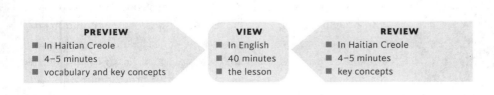

PREVIEW	VIEW	REVIEW
■ In Haitian Creole	■ In English	■ In Haitian Creole
■ 4–5 minutes	■ 40 minutes	■ 4–5 minutes
■ vocabulary and key concepts	■ the lesson	■ key concepts

FIGURE **5-1**
Preview-Review

phrases like *scratch the surface*, *I have bigger fish to fry*, or *a barrel of laughs*. Commands that are more complex can also include hands-on sequences of instructions, like following commands to make a clock out of paper plates, for example. Once learners become more proficient in their L2, they can generate their own commands for other students to perform. Understanding more complex words through TPR can be used to associate movements or gestures with their meanings. For example, teachers might create physical visuals of commands (see Figure 5-2). Recent adaptations to TPR incorporate dialogues, storytelling, role-playing, and dramatization. Because students have to demonstrate understanding by responding appropriately to commands, TPR can also be used as an informal L2 assessment.

FIGURE **5-2**
TPR Visual Scaffold

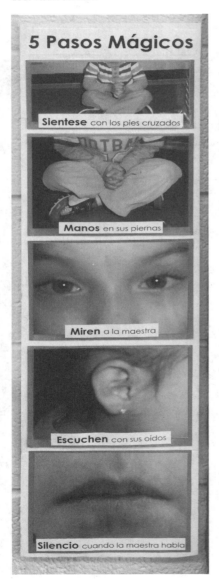

The Language Experience Approach (LEA) can be used with students at all grade levels but is most useful for beginner L2 learners and also for struggling readers. Because students provide the language used for reading instruction, the text is familiar and the concepts are of interest to them. Prior to dictating the story or narrative to the teacher, students usually participate in a shared experience, such as a science experiment, field trip, or hands-on activity that they later describe to the teacher, who records their accounts verbatim in small groups or whole class. Students are able to read their own stories with minimal difficulty because they already know the content and the meaning. In addition, students view reading and writing as purposeful communication about their own interests and concerns, because this approach is tailored to the learners' interests, background knowledge, and language proficiency level. LEA is very effective, because students engage in the reading process by using text that is familiar, concepts or ideas that are of interest, and language and vocabulary that is known.

In his second-grade dual language class, Michio uses the LEA during individual student sessions, in guided reading groups, and sometimes in whole group. When Michio did a unit on plant and animal products, he used the LEA with his entire class to demonstrate how to make butter. Michio brainstormed words and concepts with students related to dairy products and wrote them on chart paper. He then showed a glass jar, cream, and salt, and invited students to make predictions about these items, which he also wrote on the chart paper. While he was demonstrating the process of making butter, he used the think-aloud strategy. He poured the cream and salt in the jar, closed and then shook it, then passed the jar around the class as students continued to shake it. As the jar was being passed around, Michio and the students discussed their predictions and made connections to their study on animal and plant products. They were asked to observe how the contents in the jar gradually changed from liquid to solid. Once the process was complete, Michio asked students to describe their observations and the steps for making butter and wrote these on the chart paper. When the chart was complete, Michio and the students read the text together several times and later used the text for a lesson on descriptive vocabulary.

English Language Development and Sheltered Instruction

English Language Development (ELD) instruction is "designed specifically to advance English learners' knowledge and use of English in increasingly sophisticated ways . . . to help them learn and acquire English to a level of proficiency (e.g., advanced) that maximizes their capacity to engage successfully in academic studies taught in English" (Saunders, Goldenberg, and Marcelletti 2013, 14). While the main focus of ELD instruction is on language, sheltered instruction focuses on students' access to content. The authors add that when "students are being taught in a language they do not fully comprehend, instruction is 'sheltered' (or adjusted) in order to help students learn skills and knowledge in the content areas. So, while the primary goal of sheltered instruction is academic success in the content areas, the primary goal of ELD instruction is learning English" (14). Even though the emphasis of ELD is on English, the strategies and practices are applicable to LOTE as a second language in two-way dual language classroom.

Sheltered instruction scaffolds the learning process to make content accessible to L2 learners by using special techniques to help them understand and master the academic curriculum through comprehensible input in the L2. This approach involves modifications and scaffolds like breaking directions into manageable chunks and using flexible grouping to address the range of abilities and language levels in the dual language classroom. Modified instruction should maintain the rigor of lessons without simplifying the content. Teacher modifications include speaking and enunciating clearly, repeating and paraphrasing key points, and combining nonverbal communication cues (such as pictures, objects, and gestures) with spoken or written language (see Figure 5-3).

Cooperative Learning

Research findings show that students who complete learning tasks in cooperative learning groups improve their understanding of concepts at deeper levels, while increasing their motivation for learning. Studies have also found that students who engage in cooperative learning tend to have better social skills, higher self-esteem, and hold fewer stereotyped views about others (Barron and Darling-Hammond 2008).

FIGURE **5-3**
Sheltered Instruction
Teacher Modifications

Language Support	• Uses:
	» gestures, point to objects, dramatization, draw pictures
	» visuals like video clips, photos/drawings, real objects
	» verbal emphasis accompanied by writing on board
	» wait-time and extra time to complete tasks
	» clear and consistent signals for classroom instructions
	» predictable classroom routines
	• Breaks down information into smaller chunks
	• Enunciates clearly
	• Allows students to use their L1
	• Rephrases and paraphrases in shorter sentences and simpler syntax
	• Presents same information in a variety of ways
	• Provides frequent summaries and key vocabulary
	• Checks for understanding (has students demonstrate their learning)
Word Building	• Avoids idioms and contractions
	• Uses cognates, synonyms for complex vocabulary (dwelling—house)
	• Highlights words: colored sticky notes or markers, <u>underline</u>, **bold**, boxes , CAPITAL LETTERS, *italics*, *stars*

Cooperative learning provides peer support while allowing all students, regardless of their linguistic or academic levels, to participate and contribute in the learning process. In this approach, students work collaboratively in small groups on a common task to meet academic, linguistic, and social-interaction goals. Unlike other forms of group work, where students solve problems together but are only responsible for their individual learning, cooperative learning emphasizes both individual *and* collective learning of all members of the group.

Cooperative learning goes beyond just having students sitting in groups. They must work together to accomplish shared learning goals and jointly problem-solve and complete assignments or projects, which they can later apply on their own. For cooperative learning to be effective, teachers must carefully organize the group membership, make intergroup expectations clear, and facilitate collaborative activities like jigsaw, numbered-heads-together, and think-pair-share. Teachers must also incorporate three key elements: (1) academic and linguistic objectives (e.g., understanding the scientific method and using correct punctuation), (2) learning strategies (e.g., applying questioning strategies to make meaning from text), and (3) interpersonal skills (e.g., turn-taking).

Because peer interaction is essential for daily use of academic language, this approach facilitates meaningful and engaging teamwork in the dual language classroom. Students who are at different levels of academic and L2 proficiencies can help each other process information and concepts more efficiently and effectively. In addition, cooperative learning provides opportunities for students to develop cross-cultural and social skills that increase their interest and motivation while lowering the anxiety and stress associated with learning through an L2. Because students need opportunities to receive comprehensible input and practice expressive language through output, cooperative learning provides the ideal method to engage dual language students in developing their expressive and receptive academic language.

Instructional Conversations

Vygotsky suggests that teaching consists of assisted performance through a learner's zone of proximal development (ZPD) and that conversation is the most important practice in supporting learning. Instructional conversations, also known as collaborative talk, offer authentic ways for making sense of new information and linking new ideas and concepts to what students already know. Several key elements of instructional conversations distinguish them from typical classroom discussions, including a challenging but nonthreatening environment, responsiveness to student contributions, connected discourse, encouragement of discussion and participation, activation of prior knowledge, reinforcement of increasing complex language and expression, and metacognitive scaffolding.

Saunders and Goldenberg (2007) describe instructional conversations as "a way to capitalize on the teaching and learning potential of 'talk about text'" (222) that involve interesting and meaningful interactions between teacher and students, as well as among students. The difference between instructional conversations and traditional instruction is in the teacher's assumption that students have something valuable to say beyond answering questions the teacher already knows. Through instructional conversations, students try out new ways of thinking, reshape their ideas midsentence, respond instantly to others' comments, and collaborate in constructing meaning. This approach is especially effective for L2 learners, because they are actively engaged in real communication while connecting topics of interest and relevance to academic content. When instructional conversations are seen as an organized and intentional form of assisted performance, opportunities for coparticipation and coconstruction of new knowledge are enhanced in the dual language classroom.

Thematic Approach

The thematic approach works exceptionally well in dual language classrooms because students with different academic and language proficiency levels can engage in authentic learning across all content areas (Soltero 2004). This approach also helps to manage the time and scheduling demands of covering all the content areas in two languages through an integrated curriculum. The thematic approach organizes instruction, learning, and assessment around a broad topic, theme, or essential question, and is aligned to learning standards and outcomes. Rather than a collection of activities related to a topic, the thematic approach integrates language arts and content areas around broad concepts or understandings that are woven throughout the unit. Those planning thematically must consider length of units, instructional materials needed, types of activities and projects, and assessment tools.

Scaffolding Academic Oral Language

Dual language instruction needs to make use of students' prior experiences to make sense of the curriculum and understand the intersection of their two languages. Linguistically responsive instruction considers the relationship between the L1 and L2, the developmental stages of L2 acquisition, and the types of language scaffolds needed to develop oral language as the foundation for biliteracy. Research findings confirm that strong oral language in the L1 facilitates oral language in the L2 (August and Shanahan 2010). Because many L2 learners in dual language classrooms may initially lack the necessary amount of words to understand, write, and talk about academic content in the L2, their vocabulary must be built in meaningful and engaging ways.

Dual language teachers must scaffold the L2 so that students can process input (listening and reading) and also provide many opportunities for output (speaking and writing). For students with beginner and low-intermediate language proficiency levels, the L2 can only make sense when the input is adapted and supported by visual aids and context, making it comprehensible. Students acquire the L2 by understanding messages that are slightly above their current language proficiency level (Krashen 1982). Comprehensible input is supported by modifications and other types of scaffolding specifically planned for L2 learners, like breaking instruction into smaller steps, using shorter sentences that gradually build in complexity, and using graphic organizers. Comprehensible input alone is not enough for students to become fully proficient in the L2. They must also engage in a great deal of output, using the language in speaking and writing through interaction, checking for understanding, and asking for clarification (Swain 1985). Teachers can employ a variety of scaffolding supports for instruction at the same time that students themselves use them for demonstrating understanding (see Figure 5-4). Other types of scaffolds

FIGURE **5-4**
Teacher and Student Scaffolds

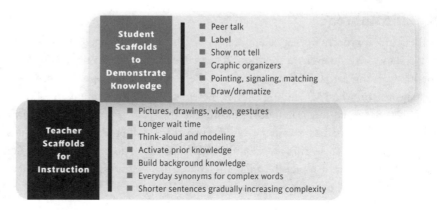

DUAL LANGUAGE EDUCATION

that support students' access to content and help them develop advanced academic skills in both languages are listed in Figure 5-5.

Strategies that support academic oral language development along with listening skills include think-alouds, where the teacher or students "show while they talk," using gestures and visuals to verbally explain new concepts, processes, or vocabulary. During think-alouds, teachers model cognitive processes as they read, write, or solve a problem through oral description. As students themselves think aloud with teachers and with each other, they gradually internalize this dialogue that eventually becomes part of their inner speech. Thinking aloud helps students engage in metacognitive processes and become aware of how they think and learn, adding to their metabilingual awareness. Labeling, chunking, and paraphrasing help students access challenging and unfamiliar material. Teachers should also provide ongoing feedback and allow sufficient wait time for students to process information and demonstrate their understanding.

Visual Scaffolds

Visual scaffolding includes illustrations, photos, gestures, film, and realia (concrete objects or artifacts) that facilitate understanding of the L2 by connecting unfamiliar words and phrases to images or objects. Scaffolds that make extensive use of visual aids are particularly useful for L2 learners in building background knowledge and vocabulary. An example of a visual scaffold is the chart in Figure 5-6 that presents a series of directions for students to follow at a writing center, which includes both print and drawings to support students' different levels of literacy and English language proficiencies.

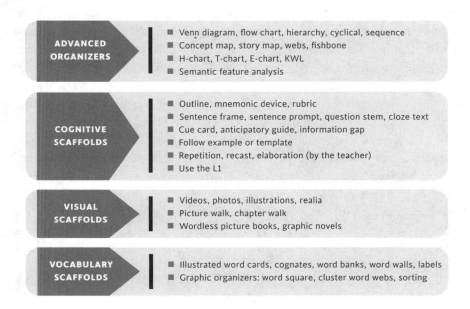

FIGURE **5-5**
Types of Scaffolds

ADVANCED ORGANIZERS
- Venn diagram, flow chart, hierarchy, cyclical, sequence
- Concept map, story map, webs, fishbone
- H-chart, T-chart, E-chart, KWL
- Semantic feature analysis

COGNITIVE SCAFFOLDS
- Outline, mnemonic device, rubric
- Sentence frame, sentence prompt, question stem, cloze text
- Cue card, anticipatory guide, information gap
- Follow example or template
- Repetition, recast, elaboration (by the teacher)
- Use the L1

VISUAL SCAFFOLDS
- Videos, photos, illustrations, realia
- Picture walk, chapter walk
- Wordless picture books, graphic novels

VOCABULARY SCAFFOLDS
- Illustrated word cards, cognates, word banks, word walls, labels
- Graphic organizers: word square, cluster word webs, sorting

FIGURE **5-6**
Scaffolds for
Language,
Literacy, and
Content

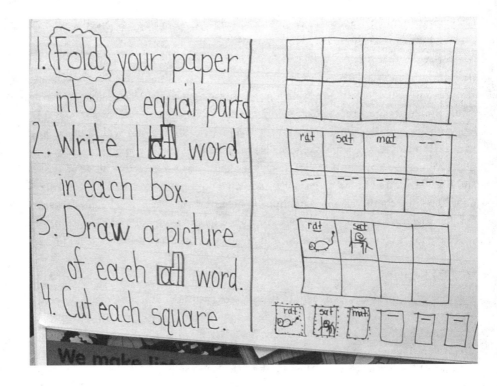

Organizational Scaffolds

The use of graphic organizers is another especially effective tool for L2 learners, because they provide a visual organizational frame for making sense of concepts without requiring extensive knowledge in the L2. Graphic organizers can be used to make connections, summarize, or sequence ideas and concepts. The most common graphic organizers include concept maps (story, pictorial, chain, cyclical, and sequential maps), semantic feature analyses, Venn diagrams, and dual concept organizers. Other graphic organizers, such as fishbone or step organizers, help students arrange, categorize, and classify knowledge. Dual concept organizers are used to represent relationships between ideas or concepts, such as cause/effect, compare/contrast, problem/solution, and fact/opinion, and are also effective strategies to help conceptualize associations or correlations between ideas. Teachers at all grade levels should ask students to select on their own the appropriate graphic organizer that corresponds to a particular purpose. For example, if students are asked to compare two concepts, they should know that they have to use a Venn diagram and not a step organizer. This helps students become strategic and independent learners.

ESL and LOTE as a Second Language (LOTE-SL)

Specialized L2 instruction is more pertinent to elementary programs, because dual language students in middle and high school have, for the most part, acquired bilingual and biliterate proficiencies. In both one-way and two-way programs, ELs must receive ESL instruction until they are reclassified as English proficient. In two-way programs, native English speakers should also receive specialized LOTE-SL instruction. For example, native English speakers in a Korean-English two-way program who are not yet proficient in their L2 should receive Korean as a second language (KSL) instruction.

Although dual language students develop most of their L2 competencies through content learning and interaction with L2 speakers, those who are at the beginner and intermediate language proficiency levels benefit from specialized targeted L2 instruction. Some argue that specialized L2 instructional periods are not necessary, because dual language students access the language while learning content subjects. There are potential problems with this view. First, federal and state laws require that ELs receive ESL instruction based on state ESL standards, so this needs to be reflected in teachers' schedules and lesson plans. Students need to acquire the L2 through ESL or LOTE-SL strategies and instructional materials that have L2 objectives, are especially designed for L2 acquisition, and are differentiated according to students' language proficiency levels. Another area of concern is the tendency for ESL to be thought of as "English language arts with modifications." This is problematic for students who are at the beginner and intermediate language proficiency levels. Using a curriculum that is designed for native English-speaking students is not appropriate for ELs who need curricular and instructional approaches specially designed for L2 learners.

In ESL or LOTE-SL, students are typically grouped homogeneously by language and receive instruction ranging from twenty to sixty minutes every day, depending on the grade and language proficiency level. Even in this language-focused ESL or LOTE-SL, the L2 should be content based, rather than only focused on discrete L2 skills. The L2 instruction emphasizes vocabulary and other linguistic aspects related to academic content. This connection between the L2 and academic content engages students in acquiring vocabulary, grammatical structures, and phonology of the L2 by understanding content concepts, developing ideas, and learning skills in both languages. For beginner and intermediate language proficiency levels, the content and instruction need to be modified but academically challenging. The academic content is not simplified or watered down. Instructional materials are rich, authentic, rigorous, and do not use simplified or controlled text. The ESL or LOTE-SL periods should be aligned to what students are learning in language arts. For example, if students are learning about main idea and supporting details in the L1 during language arts, they should not be learning about something completely different in the L2, like paraphrasing, for example. ESL or LOTE-SL can serve as both preview and review of vocabulary and content, providing scaffolds for students' academic and linguistic development in both languages.

Teachers sometimes are not sure about what L2 language forms and grammatical structures need to be taught and when. For example, when should teachers introduce irregular past tense, passive voice, or prepositions in ESL or *el subjuntivo* or *tríptongos* in Spanish as a second language? Is there a progression for teaching question words (*who, when, where, what, why, which, whose, how*) or should they be taught all at once? A lack of an L2 scope and sequence and alignment to L2 standards often leads to duplication of the same language objectives across grade levels. ESL and LOTE-SL scope and sequence of language forms can be found in language texts or can be created by districts or schools. A dedicated time for ESL/LOTE-SL must be incorporated in the weekly instruction and planned according to students' L2 proficiency levels. Using language proficiency levels helps teachers make appropriate modifications and adaptations to instructional delivery, instructional materials, and assessments.

Language Standards

The ESL standards most widely used in the United States are the WIDA (World-Class Instructional Design and Assessment) PK–12 English Language Development Standards, which are aligned to Common Core State Standards. WIDA has been adopted by thirty-six states, plus the District of Columbia and Puerto Rico. WIDA also includes PK–12 Spanish Language Standards that have been officially adopted by Puerto Rico. The three states with the highest numbers of ELs, New York, California, and Texas, are not part of the WIDA consortium but have their own ESL standards (California English Language Development Standards, New York Learning Standards for ESL, and Texas English Language Proficiency Standards).

In the WIDA Standards, features of language are organized into three categories: Discourse, Sentence, and Word/Phrase. The Discourse Level relates to linguistic complexity, such as amount, density, and structure of oral and written speech, as well as organization of ideas and variety of sentences. The Sentence Level corresponds to the grammar that includes elements like capitalization, spelling and other mechanics, as well as types and varieties of grammatical structures like passive voice and embedded clauses. The Word/Phrase Level refers to multiple meanings of words, idiomatic expressions (*raining cats and dogs*), collocations (*fully aware, bar of soap*), and general vs. specific/technical language. This categorization is very helpful in the dual language classroom, because the focus of L2 development goes beyond the vocabulary and grammar levels, to include extended discourse.

L2 proficiency standards need to be considered for planning and making appropriate adaptations to instruction, materials, and assessment according to language proficiency levels. Most ESL standards include five areas—language arts, mathematics, social science, science, and social/instruction—that each include the four language domains (listening, speaking, reading, writing) and language proficiency levels. In the past, three language proficiency levels were used (beginner, intermediate, and advanced), but most ESL standards now have five levels (entering, emerging, developing, expanding, and bridging). The WIDA Standards are based on Model Performance Indicators that include three elements: a cognitive function word that correlates to Bloom's Taxonomy (such as label, discuss, and compare), content that students are learning (such as geometric shapes and periodic table), and supports or scaffolds needed (such as graphic organizers, work in groups, and sentence frames). WIDA Standards also include useful Can-Do Descriptors that provide examples of how students can demonstrate knowledge and understanding according to each language proficiency level.

Assessment

While dual language programs are guided by the same mandated learning standards and assessments that all other school programs follow, they also have to account for more specific student learning objectives that include bilingual, biliterate, and cross-cultural competencies. Student assessments typically include mandated district and/or state tests, school-adopted measurement, and teacher-generated authentic evaluation tools. The current overemphasis on high stakes associated with standardized testing can have serious negative consequences like increased student retention, loss of school funding, school closings, and dismissal of teachers and principals. This creates a difficult environment for additive bilingual education and sometimes dissuades schools from implementing dual language programs. The current accountability trend that puts so much stock on English standardized test scores places an undue burden on dual language teachers and students.

It is important to understand that elementary dual language students score well on these types of English standardized tests, but usually after fifth or sixth grade, which correlates to the length of time it takes to develop academic L2. Norm-referenced language proficiency assessments determine language proficiency levels and are commonly used for initial identification and placement, and later as exit criteria. While these assessments are useful, they seldom provide a complete picture of students' L2 competencies in listening, speaking, reading, and writing, so it is necessary to also use classroom-based methods. Two-way programs need to include parallel LOTE assessments to determine L2 proficiency levels for native English speakers as well. Many norm-referenced tests for ELs are available in Spanish, like the *Language Assessment Scale* (LAS), the *IDEA Proficiency Test* (IPT), and *Stanford Spanish Language Proficiency Test* (SSLP). In the past ten years, more language proficiency tests have been made available in other languages besides Spanish. The Center for Applied Linguistics (CAL) offers the *Student Oral Proficiency Assessment* (SOPA) for second to eighth grade in Spanish, French, German, Japanese, and Chinese; the *Early Language Listening and Oral Proficiency Assessment* (ELLOPA) for grades PK–2 is available in Spanish, French, German, Japanese, Hebrew and Chinese; and the *CAL Oral Proficiency Exam* (COPE) for fifth to eighth grade is available in Spanish, French, German, Japanese, Russian, and Chinese. CAL also provides the Foreign Language Assessment Database directory that lists over two hundred assessments in ninety languages (http://webapp.cal.org/FLAD). Additional assessment resources include two assessments developed by the Center for Applied Second Language Studies: *Standards-Based Measurement of Proficiency* (STAMP) available in Spanish, Japanese, and Chinese, and *LinguaFolio,* an online "e-portfolio evaluation tool that allows students to collect evidence demonstrating their communicative abilities in a heritage or other target language."

An additional consideration is revising report cards to include L2 and cross-cultural learning objectives, which are not typically found in standard report cards. This can be done in one of two ways. The first is to include two columns, one for English and one for LOTE, grade every content category and subcategory in each language, and add an additional box with cross-cultural competencies for the English and the LOTE culture. The other is to just include a separate box for the four language domains in the L2 and the cross-cultural competencies.

Authentic and Performance-Based Assessment

The main purpose for assessment should be to guide instruction by measuring how well students are meeting the learning standards and by providing reliable and valid information regarding their progress. Authentic and performance-based assessment tools are most effective for dual language programs because they provide reliable data on students' acquisition of knowledge, ability to apply that knowledge, and academic growth over time in two languages. Authentic and performance-based assessments, in comparison to standardized tests, are better at measuring students' academic achievement and biliteracy skills, and provide more useful information on students' progress that can better guide instruction. Assessment processes are comprised of collection, documentation, and analysis of data on student learning. Figure 5-7 provides examples of the types of authentic and performance-based assessment tools that can be used to collect information about student learning.

Constructed Response	Product	Performance	Process-Focused
Fill in the blank	Essay	Presentation	Conference
Match	Fact sheet	Demonstration	Interview
Label a diagram	Journal	Debate	Observation
Short answer	Report	Recital	Learning log
Visual presentation:	Story	Dramatization	Process description
• Graphic organizer	Poem	Dramatic reading	Portfolio
• Diagram	Exhibit	Role play/skit	
• Flowchart	Portfolio		
• Table	Science project		
• Photographs	Model		
• PowerPoint, multimedia			
• Podcast			

FIGURE **5-7**
Authentic Assessment

Portfolios are particularly valuable in dual language programs, because they offer comprehensive long-term analysis of students' growth in both languages. Through a systematic and organized collection of student work samples, academic and language proficiency progress can be monitored over time. Especially relevant for dual language programs is the collection of written work samples in the L1 and L2 that can be compared over time, as students become fully biliterate. Students' oral speech samples, such as debates, dramatizations, and presentations, can also be collected through digital recordings or voice threads. E-portfolios provide a more efficient paperless medium to collect and store students' work and evaluations, and also make it much easier to access by the teacher at the next grade level, as well as allowing students to have copies of their own work. Several technology tools are available for teachers and students to create digital portfolios, including *Google Sites, Wikispaces, Dropbox,* and *eBackpack*.

Hybrid observation charts combine checklists or rubrics with anecdotal records that the teacher uses to guide observations, document progress, and comment on how students are understanding and mastering concepts and skills (Soltero 2004). Observation forms can be divided by academic focus (language arts, math, science, social studies), L1 and L2 development (reading, writing, listening, and speaking), or intergroup skills (such as collaboration and turn-taking). Figure 5-8 provides two examples of hybrid assessment forms. The Observation Rubric shows how the teacher documents Alexis' listening, speaking, reading, and writing development in the L2 by writing anecdotal records in each box and scoring each language domain based on a 1–5 numerical scale. The teacher observed Alexis during literacy and language arts activities in Spanish, his L2, and wrote notes on what she observed then circled the number that corresponded to his level of proficiency or achievement according to the rubric she had developed. In the second hybrid Observation Checklist

FIGURE **5-8**
Observational Assessment Forms

L1 and L2 Observation—Rubric

Name _Alexis_   Date _5-16_   Language _L2 Spanish_

LISTENING	SPEAKING
listens attentively to peers during coop. learning group activity—asks for clarification about the math learning center assignment on fractions	*uses phrases with correct voc. but sometimes mixes word order (grande libro)—requests information/ clarification often by using phases/gestures*
1 2 3 4 **(5)**	1 2 **(3)** 4 5

READING	WRITING
looks for cues in pictures—self-corrects—rereads sentences when not sure—twice substituted a word with another word that did not make sense (per for peor)	*uses phrases with inconsistent verb tense and word order—uses punctuation appropriately (periods, capitals, commas)—only uses "y" for all transitional words*
1 2 **(3)** 4 5	1 **(2)** 3 4 5

Observation—Checklist

Name _José S._   Date _3rd quarter_   Language _Math—Geometry_

☑ **2-Dimensional Figures**
    ☑ **Rhombus**
    ☑ **Parallelogram**
    ☑ **Hexagon**
    ☑ **Polygon**

☐ **3-Dimensional Figures**
    ☑ **Cube**
    ☐ **Sphere**
    ☑ **Cone**
    ☑ **Pyramid**

☐ **Attributes**
    ☑ **Edge**
    ☐ **Face**
    ☐ **Base**
    ☑ **Corner**

☑ **Symmetry**

☐ **Congruence**

3–15

uses pattern blocks to create <u>polygons</u>—matches two-dim. figures with correct term—can identify one three-dim. figure—having difficulty with cube, sphere, and differentiating between cones/pyramid while using concrete materials.

3–22

identifies almost all three-dim. figures and recognizes the difference between cone/pyramid— begins to understand the attributes of geometric figures—can apply the concept of <u>corner</u> to concrete materials and word problems

3–30

continues to have difficulty understanding sphere—identifies <u>edge</u> now and is still developing understanding of base/face—can do basic <u>symmetry</u> activities assessment chart, the teacher observed José once a week during geometry lessons in the third quarter of the year. She checked the concepts that José mastered and included observation notes on the side, dated according to each week. The teacher wrote notes about José's accomplishments and difficulties, underlining concepts he had mastered, while documenting when each skill or concept was achieved.

The most effective instructional and assessment practices for dual language classrooms are authentic and linguistically appropriate and are based on interactive, developmental, and meaningful activities. These practices better engage bilingual learners, especially when the medium of instruction is in their L2. Teachers should consider students' language proficiency levels, as well as the linguistic and cognitive demands of the curriculum, in selecting the most appropriate teaching methods that optimize their learning experiences. Likewise, assessment tools that take into account students' academic and language proficiency levels provide a more holistic view of student learning and growth.

Suggestions for Further Reading

Freeman, David, and Yvonne Freeman. 2011. *Between Worlds: Access to Second Language Acquisition*. Portsmouth, NH: Heinemann.

Horwitz, Elaine K. 2013. *Becoming a Language Teacher: Practical Guide to Second Language Learning and Teaching*. Boston: Pearson.

Wright, Wayne E. 2015. *Foundations for Teaching English Language Learners: Research, Theory, Policy, and Practice*. Philadelphia: Caslon Publishing. ✳

6

Culturally Responsive Dual Language Leadership and Program Evaluation

The ability to communicate with respect and cultural understanding in more than one language is an essential element of global competence.* . . . Language learning contributes an important means to communicate and interact in order to participate in multilingual communities at home and around the world. This interaction develops the disposition to explore the perspectives behind the products and practices of a culture and to value such intercultural experiences.

—Global Competence Position Statement,
American Council on the Teaching of Foreign Languages

---

*Global competence is a critical component of education in the 21st century, as reflected in national initiatives focused on literacy and STEM at the PK–12 level and included in the essential learning outcomes of the Liberal Education and America's Promise (LEAP) program of the Association of American Colleges and Universities (AAC&U). See more at http://www.actfl.org.

E ffective established programs are well planned, implemented, and supported. They are guided by school and district leaders who are knowledgeable about and committed to biliteracy and multiculturalism. The extent to which principals are involved in program planning, development, implementation, and improvement demonstrates their priorities and values. Principals play a critical role in the success or failure of dual language programs, because their views and attitudes shape the school climate and set schoolwide expectations for teachers, students, and families.

Creating Cross-Cultural Curriculum and Culturally Responsive Schools

Scanlan and López (2015) argue that sociocultural integration is the foundation on which to "cultivate language proficiency and support academic achievement" (27). They add that visionary leadership "recognizes that all students and families represent multiple dimensions of diversity, and that pursuing social justice requires attending to inequities that surface across these dimensions. Leading in a socially just manner means actively advocating for equity" (20). The dual language principal is responsible for creating a school culture that views students' languages and cultures as assets, promotes sociocultural integration, and nurtures a community of learning and co-operation. Developing cross-cultural competencies begins with a school climate that fosters positive intergroup relationships among all members of the school community, whether the program is a strand or schoolwide. Essential to making this happen is building understanding of the complex sociocultural, historical, and political dynamics of the two language groups. Nieto and Bode (2012) suggest that effective bilingual instruction is not simply teaching content areas in another language; rather, it is using the languages, cultures, and experiences of students in meaningful ways. They add that programs like dual language education provide powerful ways for groups who come from different linguistic and cultural backgrounds to embrace diversity while developing bilingualism and biliteracy. Nieto and Bode define multicultural education as basic education for all students that "permeates the school curriculum and instructional strategies, as well as the interactions among teachers, students, and families and the very way that schools conceptualize the nature of teaching and learning" (42). Culturally responsive education creates teaching and learning spaces to develop pride and a strong sense of identity of students' own culture, as well as an understanding and recognition of the cultures and beliefs of others.

Chapter 1 speaks to the need for creating culturally relevant and responsive curriculum that goes beyond the superficial "heroes and holidays" approach. An authentic multicultural curriculum in dual language programs will undoubtedly bring up sensitive issues like immigration, divergent values, and even religious aspects associated with the LOTE culture. For example, while the *Virgen de Guadalupe* is a religious figure, it is also an important cultural icon for Mexican heritage communities. For the Pascua Yaqui Tribe, the *Deer Dancer* ritual merges native spiritualism and Catholicism and is a deep-rooted part of Yoeme cultural identity. So the study of these topics needs to be conceptualized not as religion but as cultural aspects of the LOTE speakers. Even within the same country, traditions, beliefs, and experiences are shaped by regional differences, urban or rural origin, social class, and education background. Sleeter and Grant (2009) argue that teachers should engage students in learning complete concepts related to diverse groups, rather than isolated fragments of information or events. Multicultural education in the context of dual language should provide a forum for students and teachers to examine and challenge stereotypes, prejudice, and injustice. Part of this more in-depth multicultural education is to analyze point of view and from whose perspectives the content is presented. For example, to study Christopher Columbus from the perspective of Native Americans is quite different from the standard representation in most school texts that portrays him as an explorer, discoverer, and hero. Native Americans view Columbus as an invader who enslaved their ancestors and contributed to their demise (Bigelow and Peterson 2003).

In dual language education, students from different cultural backgrounds, ethnicities, and social classes bring to the classroom their own experiences and views, which can be both positive and negative. Students' experiences and backgrounds sometimes contribute to their own stereotypes and negative perceptions about other cultures and groups. As discussed in Chapter 2, children's and young adult literature offer authentic opportunities for students to explore diverse perspectives, sociocultural similarities and differences, and social justice. Particularly relevant for dual language are topics related to the immigrant experience, colonialism, world history, and power relations among global and local communities. For example, Nigerian author Chimamanda Adichie's "The Danger of a Single Story" (TED Talk 2009) presents a deeply compelling and transformative examination of stereotypes about groups of people constructed on the common narrative of a *single story* that is based on their origins, race, ethnicity, and social class. This powerful twenty-minute speech can be used to launch engaging and meaningful projects and thematic units around identity, prejudice, stereotypes, and how these relate to historical and current events.

Much like the emergence of hybrid languages like Spanglish when two languages coexist, the everyday contact of two or more cultural groups also creates hybrid cultures. Often heard among generation 1.5—a term to refer to people who immigrated to the United States as very young children—is that they do not fully belong in either the United States or their countries of origin. They embrace a transculture, a combination of the new and heritage cultures. This cross-cultural intersection forms the basis for first- and second-generation immigrant identity, and also for nonimmigrant, linguistically diverse populations like Native Americans and Puerto

Ricans. Hybrid cross-cultural topics need to be reflected in the dual language curriculum and used as a tool for developing cross-cultural competencies.

The language-culture connection cannot be divorced, and the cultural component in dual language programs should not take a back seat to academic and language development. The attention, promotion, funding, and advocacy that school leaders demonstrate help to nurture shared beliefs and a sense of community among all members of the school and elevate the status of the dual language program. Principals are in the unique position to shape schoolwide sociocultural integration practices and support the creation and implementation of culturally responsive curriculum.

Leadership

Sustainable dual language programs require long-term commitment, ongoing support, and adjustments in response to changes in school demographics and education policies. Findings from my work with seventeen PK–8 dual language schools over a period of nine years revealed a number of trends regarding the role of the principal in program sustainability. The most effective and sustainable programs had principals who believed in the value of bilingual education, embraced the LOTE and multiculturalism, had a long-term vision for the program, and advocated on its behalf within and outside the school. Frances, the principal at Calmeca Academy of Fine Arts and Dual Language, a neighborhood school in Chicago, embodies this leadership commitment. She was instrumental in installing a very large metal signage in the front of the building (see Figure 6-1) that clearly identifies it as a dual language

FIGURE **6-1**
Calmeca Academy of Fine Arts and Dual Language

school. The permanent installation of such a large sign in many ways signifies a permanent commitment to their dual language program. Frances shared that "after I am long gone, the sign will be on the building and others will carry the torch."

Principals in programs that endured past the first few years were knowledgeable about dual language, were directly involved with implementation and oversight of the program, and engaged all stakeholders in shared decision making. A critical indicator of school leaders' commitment is when they participate in professional development alongside their teachers. Their participation in dual language professional development ensures that everyone receives the same information so that there is common ground and shared knowledge for decision making. When the principal and other school leaders are not part of professional development, messages and information that teachers hear may be at odds with decisions made by the administration.

While support from central office administration was evident in several of the more established programs, some did not have this support and yet their programs were well implemented with positive academic and language outcomes. Principals in successful and sustainable programs shared a number of practices related to their staff: they hired motivated teachers and provided them with mentoring and support, encouraged teachers to be flexible and creative, provided time for collaboration and planning, encouraged teachers to develop ownership of the program, and offered incentives like extra time, stipends, and materials. Regarding school climate, committed principals ensured that both languages and cultures were represented throughout the school and also promoted a sense of bilingual and cultural pride among all stakeholders, even students who spoke languages other than the two used in the program. Findings from this research also point to five interconnected and interdependent organizational aspects that principals helped to facilitate and promote: cohesion, consistency, coordination, compatibility, and commitment. These "Essential 5 Cs" are particularly significant in creating high-quality dual language programs (see Figure 6-2).

The Essential 5 Cs

Cohesion refers to the extent to which all curricular areas—L1 and L2 language arts, culture, content, standards, and assessments—are connected, integrated, and aligned. Content areas and language arts should be integrated as much as possible, especially social studies with culture, reading, writing, and oral language development. For example, at Toltec Middle School dual language teachers aligned their unit plans so students had an interconnected and integrated curriculum. Sofia, the sixth-grade language arts dual language teacher, engaged her students in comparison and contrast while reading and writing about ancient civilizations. Agus, the

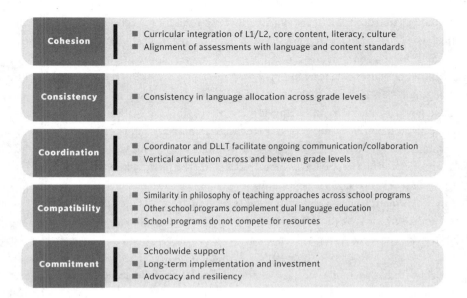

FIGURE **6-2**
The Essential 5 Cs

Cohesion
- Curricular integration of L1/L2, core content, literacy, culture
- Alignment of assessments with language and content standards

Consistency
- Consistency in language allocation across grade levels

Coordination
- Coordinator and DLLT facilitate ongoing communication/collaboration
- Vertical articulation across and between grade levels

Compatibility
- Similarity in philosophy of teaching approaches across school programs
- Other school programs complement dual language education
- School programs do not compete for resources

Commitment
- Schoolwide support
- Long-term implementation and investment
- Advocacy and resiliency

social studies teacher, had her students analyze Mayan, Chinese, and Egyptian historical milestones and contributions while the science teacher Juanma had students studying the different flora and fauna of each of these regions. Meanwhile, the math teacher Tota had students explore the differences and similarities in each of these civilizations' numeric systems. All this content-specific learning is interconnected, so students and teachers can make references to what is learned across content areas.

L2 objectives (ESL or LOTE-SL) also need to align what is being learned in language arts and content areas in the L1, especially social studies. Assessment must be aligned to the specified L1 and L2 objectives and content standards so that students are evaluated on what was learned. Cohesion in curricular areas should also be reflected in the three major components of lessons or units: L1-L2 and content learning standards/objectives are outlined; lessons, strategies, activities, and projects reflect the learning standards/objectives; and assessments measure the learning standards/objectives (see Figure 6-3).

Consistency represents the types of dual language elements that should be evident in all classrooms. These include similarities in instructional approaches and materials, student engagement, assessment methods, language color-coding, and classroom routines. While teachers must have flexibility in choosing activities, instructional

FIGURE **6-3**
Alignment Learning
Objectives—Teaching and
Assessment

L1–L2
Objectives
L–S–R–W
+ Content
Objectives

Strategies/activities/
projects include
L1–L2 Objectives
L–S–R–W
+ Content Objectives

Assess L1–L2
Objectives
L–S–R–W
+ Content
Objectives

methods, and routines, they should also follow similar types of teaching approaches that share compatible teaching orientations. For instance, students going from one grade level that uses hands-on and learner-centered approaches to the next grade level that only uses rote learning, memorization, and direct instruction would not be consistent. This lack of consistency is detrimental to students' learning and the program goals. Consistency in having authentic, engaging, and culturally responsive instructional materials also need to be reflected in all classrooms. A visitor that walks through several dual language classrooms should not see one that is full of authentic children's books, manipulatives, and student-created print, while another classroom only has workbooks, worksheets, and store-bought printed materials.

Coordination across and within grade levels helps to ensure cohesion, consistency, and continuity. Vertical articulation is done with grade levels directly below and above (for example, fifth grade articulates down with fourth and up with sixth-grade teachers) and also across grade bands (elementary with middle school, and middle school with high school). Horizontal articulation happens in grade-level meetings in elementary (for example, all the fifth grade teachers meet to plan) and department meetings in high school. These articulations help to ensure that the language allocation is followed at each grade level, cross-cultural components of the program are covered, instructional approaches and materials are in keeping with the model, and family involvement and communication efforts are shared. The principal, together with program coordinator and the Dual Language Leadership Team, facilitates this coordination.

Ensuring that there is *compatibility* among all school programs and initiatives helps to maintain overall cohesion in the school. All programs within the school, including dual language, should supplement and enhance each other, rather than compete for resources and time or be contradictory in philosophy and approach. When programs have incompatible goals and approaches, teachers become overburdened because they have to navigate and shift between conflicting practices. For example, dual language subscribes to constructivist and learner-centered pedagogy, and so it is incompatible with literacy or content programs that follow prescriptive direct-instruction approaches. Dual language educators should engage in ongoing reflection about aspects outside the program that may be at odds with its intended goals, and address conflicting or incompatible practices in program implementation. Schools with ESL and world language programs should coordinate and integrate these with dual language as much as possible.

Commitment is a tricky concept because most teachers and school leaders are dedicated and deeply involved in the profession. The type of commitment needed to create sustainable dual language programs requires additional long-term investment in training, time, effort, and funding. Advocacy is needed to guard against incompatible district and state policies and misinformed decisions that weaken dual language program goals (Genesee 2011). Principals are in unique positions to advocate for and defend their programs with central office administrators. Practices that undermine programs include high-stakes testing and districtwide adoption of instructional materials that do not align with the principles of dual language education or are designed with a monolingual and monocultural lens. Building resiliency among staff to increase teacher and principal retention is also an important part of commitment to dual language education. Given that the essential premises of dual language include long-term implementation and continuity, creating resiliency among the staff is critical for sustainability and program improvement.

Shared Decision Making

Dual language education is best implemented when all stakeholders participate in shared decision making. Teachers and families should have active roles in program development, implementation, evaluation, and improvement. Principals who encourage teachers and families—and sometimes students in the middle and high school settings—to be part of the decision-making process result in higher buy-in, ownership, and commitment (Hamayan, Genesee, and Cloud 2013). Establishing a Dual Language Leadership Team and other systems for dialogue, problem-solving, and consensus-building about implementation and improvement creates stronger programs that can withstand the various challenges that schools experience while adapting to new education mandates and initiatives.

Lil, a principal of an urban PK–8 dual language school, describes her role in promoting positive attitudes and continued support for the dual language program. As the principal of a PK–8 two-way dual language school, Lil believes that there are two key elements that result in sustainable high-quality programs: significant teacher and parent involvement in decision making, and high levels of teacher and parent satisfaction with the program. Lil, together with the Dual Language Leadership Team, discussed ways to create new procedures for student placement, new policies for attendance and homework, and report cards that included L2 benchmarks. She sought input and feedback from families and made collaborative decisions with the Dual Language Parent Council on issues that were relevant to families and the community. Lil also invited the Dual Language Leadership Team to provide feedback on curricular matters, including the selection of instructional materials and adoption of cultural enrichment programs like performance and fine arts grants. Lil often extended open invitations to teachers and families to participate on committees to talk about, problem-solve, and create action plans to address the needs of the school and program. She also created committees in response to particular areas that needed attention. For example, Lil selected a group of teachers who had attended a series of professional development sessions on assessment to develop an authentic tool for monitoring and assessing students' L2 proficiency.

Lil believes that teachers are most effective when they are actively involved in making decisions that affect their classrooms and teaching. She also is well aware that increasing pressures and demands on teachers do not create the best climate for implementing a program where students take longer to score well on English standardized tests. The general antiteacher climate has taken a toll on her teachers. Lil is responsive to their concerns and needs, so she makes every effort to support them and create a low-stress environment, giving them flexibility and many opportunities to be creative. Over the years, she has noticed a trend among other school leaders to involve teachers in creating curriculum and aligning those to new standards and to district-adopted curricular programs like technology, literacy, and STEM initiatives. While this is well intentioned, she thinks that the sheer volume of new initiatives and curricular adoptions that teachers are asked to create and align ends up overwhelming them. Instead, Lil is careful to be selective about the new initiatives and only asks teachers to consider those that most closely align with the dual language program and vision/mission of the school.

Lil also finds that families are most involved when they are satisfied with the education their children are receiving and the progress they are making. This type of parent satisfaction comes from a sense of ownership and pride in the program and the school, evidence that their children are learning and progressing linguistically, academically, culturally, and socially, as well as ongoing and open communication between home and school. The letter written by a parent to the principal (see Figure 6-4) expressing gratitude about and satisfaction with the program, is the kind of word-of-mouth message shared among families that makes the most impact in promoting the program.

Dual Language Leadership Team

A leadership team for the dual language program provides the necessary structures for informed shared decision making. The primary purpose of a Dual Language Leadership Team is to discuss, assess, and analyze issues that affect the program, as well as to consider new ideas for program improvement. The leadership team should include the program coordinator, principal or assistant principal, and grade-level (in elementary) or content area (in middle and high school) teacher representatives. Other members could include librarians, coaches, or special education teachers. Some of the tasks the Dual Language Leadership Team can undertake are to create program guidelines, design mentoring systems for new teachers, revise and update the Dual Language Handbook and school website, formulate the biliteracy criteria and selection process for Seal of Biliteracy pathway awards, and facilitate vertical articulation and coordinate program expansion from elementary to high school or

FIGURE **6-4**
A Parent Letter to the
Principal

Dear Mrs. Terra:

I wanted to thank you for your leadership and efforts to bring the Dual Language Program to Gandhi Elementary. We have enjoyed being part of the first year kindergarten class. Mrs. Torres and Mr. Fintan have presented the class material in both languages and are making it fun for everyone. Although we were a little bit reluctant in the beginning (as people sometimes are with new things), we have been extremely happy with the program. Thanks to Mrs. Torres and Mr. Fintan, our daughter has learned the kindergarten curriculum while also embracing the Spanish material. We have been so pleased with her progress on both fronts throughout the year and would highly recommend this program to any incoming families with kindergarten-age children. Both teachers went above and beyond to create special programs, such as the Hispanic Heritage Month Family Dinner and the very special end of year award celebration. These events really helped the parents to bond as well, and we are all looking forward to being together as a class next year in first grade. Please pass along our appreciation to the many folks involved in bringing this program to Gandhi and making it such a success. We are looking forward to next year!

Sincerely,
Jane's Parent

from high school to college. The Dual Language Leadership Team can also be responsible for identifying annual priorities for improvement and developing action plans to address targeted outcomes (see Figure 6-5).

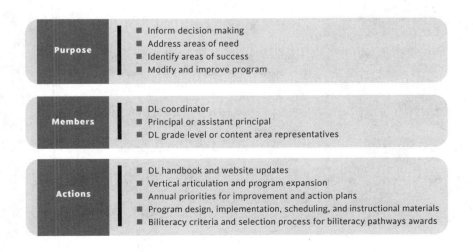

FIGURE **6-5**
Dual Language Leadership Team

Purpose
- Inform decision making
- Address areas of need
- Identify areas of success
- Modify and improve program

Members
- DL coordinator
- Principal or assistant principal
- DL grade level or content area representatives

Actions
- DL handbook and website updates
- Vertical articulation and program expansion
- Annual priorities for improvement and action plans
- Program design, implementation, scheduling, and instructional materials
- Biliteracy criteria and selection process for biliteracy pathways awards

Dual Language Program Coordinator

Principals typically provide administrative support that focuses on organizing time for planning, allocating funds and human resources, evaluating program effectiveness, and advocacy efforts. While principals also provide instructional leadership, this is usually done by a dual language coordinator who facilitates and guides instructional and programmatic aspects and oversees the implementation of the program. Coordinators are essential to program sustainability, because they function as liaisons between school leaders and teachers, as well as between school staff and families. Implementing dual language education requires flexible and systematic organizational structures, knowledgeable and competent leadership, and ongoing support and evaluation. Dual language coordinators can provide the organizational supports needed for sustainable and effective implementation. Figure 6-6 summarizes the types of responsibilities that dual language coordinators undertake to support the program, teachers, and families.

A primary task of the coordinator is to lead and organize the Dual Language Leadership Team tasked with ensuring the program is running well, enhancing the program, and engaging in problem-solving. Additional tasks include networking with other dual language schools, advocating for the program, identifying external funding sources, recruiting new students and teachers, and facilitating the annual program evaluation. The coordinator is responsible for updating the dual language

FIGURE **6-6**
Dual Language
Program Coordinator
Responsibilities

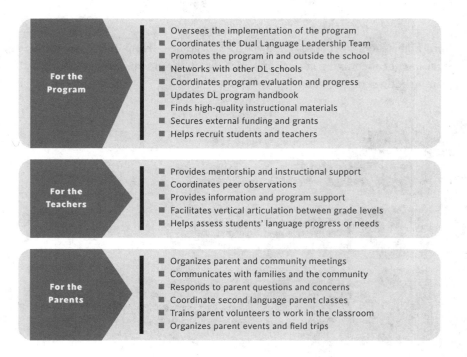

For the Program
- Oversees the implementation of the program
- Coordinates the Dual Language Leadership Team
- Promotes the program in and outside the school
- Networks with other DL schools
- Coordinates program evaluation and progress
- Updates DL program handbook
- Finds high-quality instructional materials
- Secures external funding and grants
- Helps recruit students and teachers

For the Teachers
- Provides mentorship and instructional support
- Coordinates peer observations
- Provides information and program support
- Facilitates vertical articulation between grade levels
- Helps assess students' language progress or needs

For the Parents
- Organizes parent and community meetings
- Communicates with families and the community
- Responds to parent questions and concerns
- Coordinate second language parent classes
- Trains parent volunteers to work in the classroom
- Organizes parent events and field trips

teacher and parent handbooks, as well as the dual language link on the school website. The coordinator also serves on the Dual Language Parent Council and offers support and information to families by organizing meetings, trainings, field trips, and events. In addition, the coordinator is responsible for responding to parent questions or concerns and facilitating solutions when problems arise.

Types of instructional supports that the coordinator can provide to teachers include information about L2 standards, L1 and L2 assessments, curricular expectations, and alignment of state/district mandates to the program, as well as assisting with their schedules and language allocation, and modeling lessons. In addition, the coordinator guides teachers in implementing culturally and linguistically responsive instructional approaches, strategies, and activities; locating instructional materials and other resources in both languages; and identifying appropriate L1 and L2 authentic and performance-based assessments. The coordinator should also offer instructional support to teachers through coaching, particularly mentorship to those new to dual language education. Figure 6-7 outlines four categories of key instructional elements in dual language classrooms that the coordinator can support during coaching visits. This sample observation and coaching form shows anecdotal records taken during observations of Mr. Dreux' fourth-grade social studies lesson in Haitian Creole, the discussion during the debrief between the coordinator and the teacher, and a set of recommendations.

Under *Instructional Practices*, the teacher provides interactive activities where students have ample opportunities to talk to each other in the L1 and L2. Particularly important is for students to use the LOTE for academic purposes, especially in third grade and above, when they start shifting their preference to English. While there should be no teacher code-switching, there should be evidence of cross-linguistic connections throughout the day by both teachers and students. For *Language Distribution*, the teacher and coordinator can review the schedule to ensure that the designated language allocation for that particular grade is being followed in language arts, content areas, and other aspects of instruction, such as homework. For *Materials* and *Books*, the language allocation for the particular grade level should be reflected in the language of the materials in the classroom. For example, if the high school history teacher is designated to teach in the LOTE, then all the instructional materials and books should be in that language. In elementary grades, for example, by fifth grade the language allocation is 50-50 so the self-contained classroom materials and books should be half in English and half in the LOTE. Classrooms should be well equipped with books that are culturally relevant and authentic, both in English and the LOTE. Also, print in the two languages should be color-coded so that students can easily distinguish between them. Because the LOTE and English are situated within a global context, maps are important in dual language classrooms so that students develop geographic knowledge about where

DUAL LANGUAGE CLASSROOM OBSERVATION AND FEEDBACK

Name _Mr. Dreux_ **Content Area** _Social Studies (SS)_ **Language of Instruction** _Haitian Creole (HC)_ **Date** _1/30/2016_ **Grade** _4th_

	Observed	Teacher Comments and Debrief	Recommendations
INSTRUCTIONAL PRACTICES • Interactive • Student-to-student talk • Higher-order thinking • Cross-linguistic connections • No teacher code-switching (CS) • Students use LOTE	• mostly direct instruction • students interacting using mostly HC, some CS • praise given for using HC • no teacher CS, all HC • small word wall with cognates	• use anticipatory set in groups in English as preview-review • after lesson students did think-pair-share and a numbered-heads-together • Venn diagram in HC	• cooperative learning groups, compare/contrast Haitian and American revolutions • include cross-linguistic charts with difference/similarities in grammar construction between English-HC
LANGUAGE DISTRIBUTION • Language Arts (LA) • Content areas • Homework	• SS integrated with LA in writing/listening in comparison/contrast and related transition words • homework all in English	• no students need LOTE-SL because all are proficient in HC	• allocate balanced language of homework by week
MATERIALS • Reflects language % • Languages color-coded • Technology LOTE/English • Classroom print LOTE/English • Maps	• classroom print half in HC and half in English • color-coding on some charts but not others (HC red, English black) • no map displayed • technology only used in English	• maps have been removed, teacher uses SMART Board to project maps when relevant but this takes time so does not often do it • limited access to quality technology programs in HC	• display a world map to refer to Haiti and French-speaking countries/regions • make color-coding consistent • DLLT will identify HC technology tools and supplemental materials
BOOKS • LOTE/English • Cultural/authentic	• more books in English than HC, but significantly more HC than last year • limited HC culture reflected in reading materials	• limited access to books in HC, have to translate reading materials • needs more authentic HC cultural reading materials	• DLLT will identify HC books and authentic cultural materials and work with Haitian Consulate and other community organizations
ESL (+LOTE-SL for 2-Way) • Daily • Curriculum or program • Language standards LOTE/ESL • Differentiate by level	• did not observe ESL curriculum, materials, or standards	• half students are intermediate/advanced level ELLs but no ESL period or standards • not sure how to integrate ESL in schedule and how to group students	• daily targeted ESL • ESL standards differentiated by language level • identify/purchase ESL materials

Note: Some features may not be observed but should be discussed during debriefing with teacher.

FIGURE **6-7**
Sample Dual Language Classroom Observation and Feedback

the two languages are used in the world. Under _ESL_ (and _LOTE-SL_ for two-way programs) there should be consistent and structured L2 instruction that follows ESL and L2 standards and language objectives, instruction that is differentiated according to students' language proficiency levels, and curriculum and materials that are designed for L2 learners. For students who are fully proficient in both languages, especially in middle and high school programs, there is no need to include ESL and LOTE-SL. The form in Figure 6-7 can be revised to include other program elements and omit those that may not be relevant.

Resource Allocation

Principals, especially in dual language strands and in high school, face many competing demands from other programs and initiatives. So school leaders must prioritize budget expenditures and how to allocate existing and new resources. Given the limited resources that most schools have, the cost of implementing a dual language program is a concern for school leaders and teachers. Dual language planning and implementation costs depend on several factors that include the current state of the school's resources, budget, and qualifications/knowledge of the staff. For instance, if school and classroom libraries are already well stocked with high-quality books and media in both languages, less funding is needed in this area. If the school previously allocated funds for professional development, there is no need to spend additional money, but shift the focus of the training. Schools that have a good track record in offering effective programs already allocate their budgets to areas that support students' academic, linguistic, and sociocultural development. For example, schools that have flexibility in how they allocate their budgets may reduce nonclassroom personnel (such as coaches and other support staff) to create smaller class sizes. Others may allocate funding for after-school support, bilingual books and instructional materials, professional development, stipends for curricular planning, enrichment programs, and family involvement. Dual language programs require no more and no less than what is expected to be spent for any high-quality program. When possible, additional funds should be earmarked for cultural educational experiences such as artists in residence, authors, musicians, cultural ensembles, and other enriching artistic and cultural resources that support the academic, linguistic, and cultural goals of the program.

Teacher Recruitment, Retention, and Strategic Hiring Practices

Principals need to be strategic in hiring when positions become vacant. Because dual language teachers must have high levels of academic language proficiency in the LOTE and also be highly qualified in their content area(s) and in bilingual and ESL pedagogy, school leaders and district administrators should have a plan for identifying, recruiting, and retaining them. Total immersion models require bilingual teachers in the early grades because the majority of the instruction is in the LOTE. Once the language allocation reaches 50-50 by fourth or fifth grade, bilingual and monolingual English speaking teachers can team-teach, which also applies to partial immersion models at all grade levels. It is important to consider the qualifications of the current teachers in a school to determine the viability of starting a program. A school that has very few bilingual teachers would first need to increase their numbers over a period of time as existing teachers retire or leave the school. One obstacles in starting a dual language program is the fear from monolingual English-speaking teachers that they will lose their positions because they are not bilingual. Dual language programs should never be implemented on the condition that any teacher in the school would lose his or her job.

Recruiting and retaining qualified bilingual teachers and school leaders often proves to be quite challenging, especially in smaller urban and suburban areas. Both long-term and short-term strategies for teacher recruitment and retention need to be considered for program sustainability. Establishing partnerships with teacher preparation institutions helps to build the dual language teacher pool and workforce capacity by increasing the number of licensed and endorsed bilingual teachers and school leaders. University students can complete their student teaching, leadership internships, and field experiences in schools with dual language programs, and in that way grow the number of school leaders and teachers who are knowledgeable about this additive bilingual model. A strategic first step is to create relationships with key university contacts, student teaching directors and teacher education faculty. Schools and district human resources offices must engage in ongoing communication with universities about specific needs for bilingual teachers, share vacancy posts, and request student teaching and field experience placements. Schools that are known for being inclusive and supportive tend to attract the most qualified and experienced dual language teachers and are more successful at recruiting and retaining committed teachers and school leaders. When existing teachers leave the school for personal reasons (retirement or relocation) or professional reasons (promotion or further education), principals should have a *replacement strategy* that involves filling these vacant positions with teachers who have a demonstrated interest, background, and qualifications in dual language education.

When the budget allows, districts sometimes subsidize partial or full tuition for teachers to earn bilingual or ESL endorsements, often requesting a three- to five-year commitment to stay in a designated school. Districts and schools can apply for federal or state grants specifically aimed at increasing the number of dual language, bilingual, or world language teachers. An alternative for districts is to recruit bilingual teachers from other states or from abroad. States that have larger populations of LOTEs, such as Arabic speakers in Michigan, Chinese speakers in California, Spanish speakers in Texas, and Haitian Creole speakers in Florida, can be good sources of bilingual teachers. More states have reciprocity regarding teacher licensure, so it has become easier to attract licensed teachers from other states. Districts increasingly recruit teachers from other states, especially during national education conferences such as those hosted by Teachers of English to Speakers of Other Languages (TESOL) and the National Association for Bilingual Education (NABE).

Recruiting and hiring bilingual teachers from abroad is more complicated and involved. This process usually happens through programs like the Fulbright Teacher Exchange Program or official agreements with foreign governments. In the last decade and a half, the process of securing work visas has become stricter and more expensive, so districts need to pay close attention to the high fees associated with applications of H-1B nonimmigrant foreign worker visas. Working through embassies or local consulates may facilitate the process if the city or state has formalized partnerships. For example, Spain's Ministry of Education offers an exchange visitor teacher program that has partnered with Illinois, Iowa, and Wisconsin. While hiring bilingual teachers from abroad has benefits, there are also drawbacks. Bilingual teachers from abroad are usually in short-term contracts, and therefore do not solve the long-term teacher shortage. It is well documented in the literature that high teacher turnover negatively affects student achievement, especially in low-income schools (Ronfeldt, Loeb, and Wyckoff 2013). For dual language education, high levels of teacher and principal turnover weakens programs. In addition, the learning curve for teachers from abroad is quite steep. By the time they start to understand all the expectations, requirements, and norms of schooling in the United States, their contracts have ended. For these foreign teachers to be successful, districts and schools must consider careful recruitment of candidates that best fit the school's philosophy and student population, long-term contracts, intensive and ongoing mentoring and support, and professional development.

Networking and Support

Networking with other dual language schools is particularly helpful for new and established programs alike. These networks can offer support in sharing knowledge, information, ideas, strategies, and resources, as well as offer solutions to problems that other programs may have experienced. Social media and new technologies make it easier to establish these networks across the United States and also transnationally. In addition, sites like *Pinterest*, *LinkedIn*, *Edmodo*, and *WeAreTeachers* can be tailored to dual language interests and needs. This is very useful for sharing and receiving information about new research, professional development opportunities, and new technology tools. For dual language principals, networking can provide much-needed support systems for issues that schools without dual language programs do not experience. These types of networking groups can organize summer institutes or retreats where all teachers and principals come together to discuss and offer solutions to areas that are challenging or ineffectual, and exchange ideas about program elements that are working well. Another option is for dual language principals to come together and form school leader consortiums to support each other and collectively advocate for their programs to district administrators, school board members, and state officials.

In Chicago, twelve dual language school principals formed the first of its kind Dual Language Principal Consortium, established to cultivate systems of support and networking, and build community among dual language school leaders. With guidance from the district's Office of Language and Culture and me as a university partner, the twelve principals have engaged in multiple collaborative efforts to share challenges and successes as they implement dual language programs in their respective schools. The Dual Language Principals Consortium members participate in a number of activities that support their efforts to continually improve their dual language programs. The principals attend quarterly leadership meetings and participate in dual language principal retreats where they share accomplishments and collectively engage in problem-solving. The principals participate in ongoing dialogues about areas of concern and ways to address internal and external challenges, including: lack of language assessments in the target language; misuse of English language standardized assessments for ELs; challenges in finding and hiring quality bilingual teachers; identifying quality, authentic, and appropriate target language instructional materials including technology tools; elevating district administrators' knowledge about and support for dual language education; creating pipelines to continuing students' language development in high school and beyond; and promoting and integrating the Seal of Biliteracy pathways recognitions. The principals created a statement of Essential Requirements and Action Items for dual language programs and formulated the Dual Language Position Statement that partially states:

> *The Dual Language Principal Consortium believes that multilingual and cross-cultural education provides all students the means to attain academic excellence in more than one language. Dual language programs foster an appreciation of language and culture with a focus on students becoming contributing members and leaders of a global society. We believe that high-quality, sustainable, and effective research-based dual language education programs are essential for students to develop the highest levels of biliteracy, academic achievement, and cross-cultural competencies. Dual language education must be offered in comprehensive, well-articulated programs guided by committed and knowledgeable teachers and school leaders. Dual language teachers must be highly qualified in their language proficiency, cultural knowledge, content knowledge and bilingual and second language teaching practices. To become a multicultural and multilingual competent society, educators and policy makers must make long-term sustainable commitments to expand language study opportunities for all students.* (Chicago Public Schools Dual Language Principal Consortium 2016)

Program Evaluation

Dual language programs should not be prescribed, prepackaged, or follow a one-size-fits-all model where school leaders and teachers are handed down prescriptive directions to follow year after year. Instead, they are based on program frameworks that are periodically evaluated and readjusted according to schools' needs, goals, and changing circumstances. Program evaluation provides the necessary information to analyze and recalibrate the program. Periodic reviews are critical for reflecting on program progress, successes, and challenges. Such evaluations are also systems for checks and balances to ensure that programmatic goals are being met. Based on these ongoing program self-assessments, goals may be added or modified each year, depending on the needs of the school and/or changes in district and state mandates. This process allows teachers, parents, and school leaders to examine and build on what has been accomplished and reformulate problematic areas or elements that have not yet been developed.

A program evaluation form can be supplemented with routine yearly school reports that include accomplishments, challenges, needs, and areas for improvement. Sometimes, evaluations are based on features outlined in the school improvement plan. Once the annual program evaluation is completed, the Dual Language Leadership Team, in consultation with the rest of the dual language teachers and support staff, should engage in a reflective analysis regarding factors that contributed to successes and challenges, and from these formulate a plan of action to address areas that need improvement. Understanding what obstacles impede effective program implementation helps to identify potential solutions and create a plan of action. These types of evaluative processes offer direct and continual analysis and reflection on program progress and needs. In addition, data collection over a period of several years can more accurately demonstrate program effectiveness and student achievement.

Figure 6-8 is an example of a program evaluation with a number of categories and criteria that come directly from the program's goals and objectives. Rating methods can vary according to the needs and preferences of each school. This example provides a basic and user-friendly rating system that reflects the extent to which the program has implemented its goals and objectives each year. The evaluation process should include all program stakeholders. After teachers, school leaders, and parents have evaluated each programmatic component, the Dual Language Leadership Team can facilitate a reflective analysis about goals that have been partially implemented or not implemented at all, and how these will be addressed the following year. Figure 6-9 is a sample plan of action for addressing areas that need improvement. Assessment tools that measure students' academic and linguistic achievement must also be part of program evaluation. Another helpful tool to conduct program evaluations

FIGURE **6-8**
Yearly Program Evaluation
and Needs Assessment

Indicate to what extent each program element has been implemented: **1 = Full   2 = Partial   3 = None**

DL STUDENTS

1	2	3	Students stay in the program at least six years.
1	2	3	Students from both language groups are integrated at least 50% of the time (2-W).
1	2	3	Data is gathered on students' academic and language development and progress.
1	2	3	Support for struggling students is offered in the L1 and/or L2.
1	2	3	Students have opportunities for interaction with non-dual language classrooms (strand).
1	2	3	Students understand the benefits of being bilingual, biliterate, and cross-cultural.
1	2	3	Students' work in two languages is displayed in the classroom and school.
1	2	3	Students' progress in the L2 is celebrated and recognized.

DL TEACHERS

1	2	3	Teachers participate in grade-level or content area meetings.
1	2	3	Teachers participate in vertical articulation with other grade levels.
1	2	3	Teachers attend weekly dual language grade-level meetings.
1	2	3	Teachers have opportunities to visit other dual language classrooms and schools.
1	2	3	Teachers and support staff attend professional development (PD) related to dual language.
1	2	3	Teachers do not translate or code-switch.
1	2	3	New dual language teachers are mentored and have additional PD opportunities.

DL FAMILIES AND COMMUNITY

1	2	3	There are systems for two-way communication between families and school.
1	2	3	Families and community are invited to share their knowledge and expertise.
1	2	3	Parents attend monthly dual language meetings.
1	2	3	Parents participate in training to support their children at home in developing the two languages.

DL INSTRUCTION AND CURRICULUM

1	2	3	The DL program is compatible with other school programs.
1	2	3	The curriculum is constructivist, learner-centered, and literature-based.
1	2	3	The curriculum is culturally responsive and relevant to the student population.
1	2	3	Metalinguistic and cross-linguistic connections are made consistently.
1	2	3	Instruction uses cooperative learning, thematic approach, inquiry-based, sheltered, and hands-on.
1	2	3	Instruction focuses on language/literacy, content knowledge, critical thinking, problem solving.
1	2	3	Authentic/performance-based assessments are used to evaluate language and academic progress.

DL INSTRUCTIONAL MATERIALS

1	2	3	World map or maps of LOTE country(ies) is displayed in every classroom.
1	2	3	Classroom libraries have authentic high-quality LOTE literature.
1	2	3	Classrooms have sufficient LOTE books and print resources.
1	2	3	Technology materials in the LOTE are interactive and engaging.
1	2	3	Classroom print reflects the language allocation of the grade level.

DL LEADERSHIP

1	2	3	A DL coordinator provides administrative and curricular support.
1	2	3	Sufficient funding is allocated for the program.
1	2	3	The DL Leadership Team meets monthly.
1	2	3	The school library is increasing its bilingual/multicultural collection.
1	2	3	School leaders attend PD and education conferences related to dual language.
1	2	3	The principal provides time for teachers to plan with each other and with other dual language schools.
1	2	3	The district supports the implementation of the dual language program.

FIGURE **6-9**
Priorities for Improvement
and Action Plan

Identify a programmatic goal that has been partially ❷ or not implemented ❸ (from Annual Program Evaluation).
Describe obstacles that prevent implementation, possible solutions, action steps, and timeline to address implementation of the goal.

	PROBLEM	SOLUTION	ACTION	TIMELINE
DL STUDENTS				
2 Students' work in two languages is displayed in the classroom and school.	• lack of classroom wall space • cannot attach displays on painted walls	• install pin strips in rooms/halls • designate at least ¼ of the wall space to display student work	• order and install pin strips, then display student work	1–2 months
DL TEACHERS				
2 New DL teachers are mentored and have additional PD opportunities.	• no mentoring program • lack of time	• provide time for sharing, planning, peer observation, and networking • create a mentoring plan	• establish a buddy system • assign a master teacher or coordinator for mentoring • DLLT creates mentoring plan	1 year
DL FAMILIES and COMMUNITY				
3 Parents attend monthly DL meetings.	• few parents attend parent meetings • newsletter is not sent out consistently	• increase interest and access to parent meetings • incorporate DL news in the school newsletter and website	• alternate day and night meetings and present fun and relevant topics • coordinator updates newsletter and website with DL news	2–3 months
DL INSTRUCTION and CURRICULUM				
3 The curriculum is culturally responsive and relevant to the student population.	• curriculum not aligned to LOTE culture/history • few instructional materials reflect LOTE culture/history	• include connections to LOTE culture/history in curriculum • create LOTE culture units • identify culturally relevant materials for curriculum	• grade-level teams integrate curriculum and develop new units after school and summer • locate/purchase culturally relevant materials for new units	1 year
DL INSTRUCTIONAL MATERIALS				
3 A world map or map of the LOTE countries is visible at all times.	• almost no classrooms have physical maps of LOTE countries • limited connections to geography of LOTE	• purchase world or LOTE maps for every classroom to supplement digital atlas and maps	• utilize map daily to connect LOTE content to geography • engage students in study of geography about the US and LOTE countries	2–3 months
DL LEADERSHIP				
2 Sufficient funding is allocated for the program.	• budget cuts • funds spent on other programs	• allocate percentage of budget for the program • seek grants	• identify one/two priorities per year and fund those	1 year

is the *Guiding Principles for Dual Language Education*, developed by the Center for Applied Linguistics, that offers a comprehensive and detailed range of components organized in seven strands: assessment and accountability, curriculum, instruction, staff quality and professional development, program structure, family and community, and support and resources. Each strand includes a number of principles that provide detailed descriptions of programmatic elements.

Challenges Implementing Sustainable Dual Language Programs

Demographic changes in school student population, pressures from high-stakes testing in English, lack of district support, limited access to professional development, insufficient quality bilingual instructional materials, and shortage of qualified bilingual teachers are among some of the challenges that schools encounter in implementing dual language programs. Teachers may become ambivalent or even opposed to dual language education because of the increasing pressures for high scores in English standardized tests. School principals have the responsibility to make sure that teachers and other school staff are fully committed to the program and understand the delayed payoff and benefits of teaching and learning in two languages. Moreover, the principal must also ensure that this is understood by district administrators and their board of education members. In some schools, there are teachers who simply do not believe in bilingual education, and who can have serious detrimental effects on the program and undermine its effectiveness. It falls to the principal to communicate a shared and agreed-upon stance regarding additive bilingualism and viewing students' languages and cultures as assets to be further developed. Teachers and other school staff who do not agree with these tenets are certainly entitled to their beliefs but are not a good match for schools with dual language programs.

Families can also sometimes reject bilingual education and demand English-only instruction. This calls for teachers and school leaders to provide information and opportunities to voice their concerns. An effective approach to ease families' concerns about the program is to ask the Dual Language Parent Advisory Council, or parents who are very satisfied with the program, to share their positive experiences. Another strategy is to invite parents to visit dual language classrooms so that they can see for themselves the supportive and positive learning environments in which their children participate.

Changing demographics affect both student recruitment, something that is especially challenging for two-way programs, and qualified bilingual teacher recruitment. Student mobility and attrition affect efforts to maintain balanced representation of students from both language groups in two-way models. Parents should understand that transferring their children in and out of the program will have adverse effects on their academic and biliteracy development. Programs that see a demographic shift where the majority of students speak the LOTE can implement a one-way model and offer world language classes in the LOTE. On the other hand, dual language programs that struggle to attract native LOTE-speaking students should have a recruitment plan that includes partnering with area preschools, child care centers, and other community organizations to make the program known to the community and attract their LOTE-speaking children. LOTE social media, print media, and local television and radio can also be effective in recruiting LOTE-speaking children.

Dual language education is not simple or easy to implement. Most dual language programs will experience difficulties and stumbling blocks along the way. The key is for school leaders, teachers, families, and the community to work together to ensure dual language programs thrive in light of these challenges. Throughout the chapters in this book, I offer the foundational knowledge, research-based information, and comprehensive guidelines required to design, plan, and implement high-quality and sustainable dual language programs. Today's PK–12 student population comes to school with a variety of languages, cultures, backgrounds, and experiences. We are also in an era of increasing global demand for a more highly educated, bilingual, and biliterate workforce. These two realities compel educators and policy makers to offer more culturally and linguistically responsive education that speaks to this diversity and these demands. In particular, teachers and school leaders are challenged to identify ways to provide expanded academic and linguistic skills for all students to have full participation in a variety of educational, social, linguistic, cultural, and economic contexts. For culturally and linguistically diverse students, dual language education offers the best alternative to increase their academic achievement and to boost their social and economic potentials. In turn, dual language education is an attractive option for native English speakers to participate in an extended bilingual education experience so that they, too, can benefit from reaching bilingual, biliterate, and cross-cultural competencies. Lindholm-Leary (2012) contends that "merely adopting the DLE name and some components of the model will not necessarily result in successful student outcomes. Rather, successful outcomes require a clear understanding of the DLE program and full implementation of the various characteristics associated with high-quality programs" (261). Sustainable high-quality programs are driven by leadership practices that build on the strengths of the community, teachers, and students.

Suggestions for Further Reading

Miramontes, Ofelia B., Adel Nadeau, and Nancy L. Commins. 2011. *Restructuring Schools for Linguistic Diversity: Linking Decision Making to Effective Programs.* New York: Teachers College Press.

Nieto, Sonia, and Patty Bode. 2012. *Affirming Diversity: The Sociopolitical Context of Multicultural Education.* Boston: Pearson.

Scanlan, Martin, and Francesca A. López. 2015. *Leadership for Culturally and Linguistically Responsive Schools.* New York: Routledge.

Soltero, Sonia W. 2011. *Schoolwide Approaches to Educating ELLs: Creating Linguistically and Culturally Responsive K–12 Schools.* Portsmouth, NH: Heinemann.

Wagner, Susan, and Tamara King. 2013. *Implementing Effective Instruction for English Language Learners: 12 Key Practices for Administrators, Teachers, and Leadership Teams.* Philadelphia: Caslon Publishing.

Glossary of Acronyms

M any terms and acronyms are used in the field of second language education. Below is a brief list of terms used in the field.

STUDENTS		
Bilingual Learner	BL	Term I use to refer to students who are bilingual or becoming bilingual. Includes ELs and native English speakers
English Learner	EL	Widely used term. May be perceived as too focused on English, rather than bilingual nature of ELs.
Dual Language Learner	DLL	Recent term used in early childhood education to refer to ELs. May be confusing because it is a term associated with dual language programs.
Emergent Bilingual	EB	Recent term used to refer to the bilingual nature of ELs. Can also include native English speakers.
Limited English Proficient	LEP	Used by the government. No longer used by language educators due to negative connotation of "limitations."
Students with Interrupted Formal Education	SIFE	Older ELs who have had limited or no schooling, typically refugees or students from rural areas.
LANGUAGE		
First Language	L1	Also known as native language or mother tongue.
Second Language	L2	Students' second language.
Language Other than English	LOTE	Replaces the term "minority language."
Language Other than English or Spanish	LOTE-S	Used for all other languages beside English/Spanish.
Target Language Partner Language	TL PL	Used mostly in dual language education to refer to students' L2.
Heritage Language	HL	Language of students' heritage that they may no longer speak/understand.
English Language Development	ELD	Used in ESL standards.
PROGRAMS		
Dual Language Education Dual Language Program Two-Way Immersion	DLE DLP TWI	Additive programs that develop two languages.
Transitional Bilingual Education	TBE	Subtractive programs that include L1 instruction (plus ESL) typically 3–4 years when ELs transition to all English classrooms.

(continued)

PROGRAMS		
Partial Immersion	50-50	50% time instruction in the LOTE and 50% in English throughout the program.
Full Immersion	80-20 90-10	Initially the majority of instruction in elementary school is in the LOTE, increasing to reach balanced instruction in both languages by 4th or 5th grade.
One-Way Dual Language	1-way	All students from the same language, typically ELs.
Two-Way Dual Language	2-way	Students include ELs and native English speakers.
Team-Teaching (Side-by-Side)	TT	Two teachers instruct students, typically one bilingual in the LOTE and the other monolingual in English.
Self-Contained (Roller-Coaster)	SC	One bilingual teacher instructs in both languages.
English as a Second Language	ESL	Instructional program for ELs based on ESL standards and ESL strategies. Part of bilingual and dual language programs.
LOTE as a Second Language	LOTE-SL	The same as ESL but in the LOTE. Instruction for English native speakers in their L2.
Spanish as a Second Language	SSL	Spanish as a second language. Other LOTEs: ASL—Arabic as a Second Language, or CSL—Chinese as a Second Language, etc.

Resources and Professional Organizations

Organizations and Research Centers		
ATDLE	Association of Two-Way & Dual Language Education	http://atdle.org
ACTFL	American Council on the Teaching of Foreign Languages	www.actfl.org
CAL	Center for Applied Linguistics	www.cal.org
CARLA	Center for Advanced Research on Language Acquisition	http://carla.umn.edu
CERCLL	Center for Educational Resources in Culture, Language, and Literacy	http://cercll.arizona.edu
DLENM	Dual Language Education of New Mexico	www.dlenm.org
NABE	National Association for Bilingual Education	www.nabe.org
NADLL	New America's Dual Language Learners National Work Group	www.edcentral.org/tag/dual-language-learners-national-work-group
NCELA	National Clearinghouse for English Language Acquisition	www.ncela.us
NFLRC	National Foreign Language Resource Center	www.nflrc.org
TESOL	Teachers of English to Speakers of Other Languages	www.tesol.org
OELA	Office of English Language Acquisition	www2.ed.gov/about/offices/list/oela/index.html
AELRC	Assessment and Evaluation Language Resource Center	http://aelrc.georgetown.edu
	Seal of Biliteracy	http://sealofbiliteracy.org

Conferences	
La Cosecha Dual Language Conference	See www.dlenm.org
National Two-Way Conference	See http://atdle.org
National Association for Bilingual Education Conference	See www.nabe.org
Summer CARLA Institute for Second Language Teachers	www.carla.umn.edu/institutes/index.html

Catalogs

Lectorum	http://catalog.lectorum.com/search.htm
MantraLingua	http://usa.mantralingua.com
Lee and Low Books	www.leeandlow.com
Del Sol Books	www.delsolbooks.com
Multilingual Books	www.multilingualbooks.com/children.html
East West Discovery Press	www.eastwestdiscovery.com
Star Bright Books	www.starbrightbooks.org
Cinco Puntos Press	www.cincopuntos.com/bilingual.sstg
Lorito Books	http://loritobooks.com/
Language Lizard	www.languagelizard.com
Cuatrogatos	www.cuatrogatos.org
Benchmark Education	www.benchmarkeducation.com
Velazquez Press	https://velazquezpress.com

Films and Videos

Speaking in Tongues	http://speakingintonguesfilm.info
	http://blogs.edweek.org/edweek/learning-the-language/2013/09/dual_language_students_make_ca.html
Pasadena Mandarin DL Immersion at Field Elementary	www.youtube.com/watch?v=oEiEEe4nJk8
El Paso High School DL Magnet	www.youtube.com/watch?v=TQz2jVQ33oU
Broadway Elementary Mandarin Immersion	www.youtube.com/watch?v=DkpQUgUyFNA
The Importance of a DL Education	www.youtube.com/watch?v=i-TMa8ZObl4
Dallas ISD Two-Way DL	www.youtube.com/watch?v=n4OYeymmd8Q
2nd-Grade Student in Spanish DL Immersion	www.youtube.com/watch?v=co6r2fTB6wY
Beyond Ni Hao: Immersive Chinese in NY Public Schools	www.youtube.com/watch?v=NBQWtAmTVJ0
Classroom Videos (sample lessons)	www.colorincolorado.org/videos/classroom-video
Chimamanda Ngozi Adichie: The Danger of a Single Story	www.ted.com/talks/chimamanda_adichie_the_danger_of_a_single_story.html

Other Internet Sites and Blogs of Interest

Colorín Colorado	www.colorincolorado.org
¡Chispa! DL Education	www.scoop.it/t/dual-language-education
Guiding Principles for DL Education	www.cal.org/twi/Guiding_Principles.pdf
Guidelines for Implementing the Seal of Biliteracy	www.actfl.org/sites/default/files/pdfs/SealofBiliteracyGuidelines_0.pdf
North American Academy of the Spanish Language	www.anle.us

REFERENCES

Aardema, Verna. 1992. *Why Mosquitoes Buzz in People's Ears*. London, England: Puffin Press.

Andrews-Goebel, Nancy. 2002. *The Pot that Juan Built*. New York: Lee & Low Books.

Arias, Beatriz, and Milagros Morillo-Campbell. 2008. "Promoting ELL Parental Involvement: Challenges in Contested Times." Policy Brief. *The Great Lakes Center for Education Research & Practice* 3–22.

Argueta, Jorge 2005. *Xochitl and the Flowers; Xochitl, la Niña y las Flores*. San Francisco, CA: Children's Book Press.

August, Diane, and Timothy Shanahan. 2010. "Effective English Literacy Instruction for English Language Learners." In *Improving Education for English Learners: Research-Based Approaches*, 209–49. Sacramento, CA: California Department of Education.

Bak, Thomas, Jack J. Nissan, Michael M. Allerhand, and Ian J. Deary. 2014. "Does Bilingualism Influence Cognitive Aging?" *Annals of Neurology* 75 (6): 959–63.

Baker, Colin. 2011. *Foundations of Bilingual Education and Bilingualism*. Buffalo, NY: Multilingual Matters.

———. 2014. *A Parents' and Teachers' Guide to Bilingualism*. Buffalo, NY: Multilingual Matters.

Banks, James. 2015. *Cultural Diversity and Education: Foundations, Curriculum, and Teaching*. Boston: Pearson.

Barron, Brigid, and Linda Darling-Hammond. 2008. "How Can We Teach for Meaningful Learning?" In *Powerful Learning: What We Know About Teaching for Understanding,* edited by Linda Darling-Hammond, Brigid Barron, P. David Pearson, Alan H. Schoenfeld, Elizabeth K. Stage, Timothy D. Zimmerman, Gina N. Cervetti, Jennifer L. Tilson, and Milton Chen, 11–71. New York: Jossey-Bass.

Beeman, Karen, and Cheryl Urow. 2012. *Teaching for Biliteracy: Strengthening Bridges between Languages*. Philadelphia: Caslon Publishing.

Bialystok, Ellen. 2011. "Reshaping the Mind: The Benefits of Bilingualism." *Canadian Journal of Experimental Psychology* 65 (4): 229–35.

Bialystok, Ellen, Fergus Craik, and Gigi Luk. 2012. "Bilingualism: Consequences for Mind and Brain." *Trends in Cognitive Sciences* 16 (4): 240–50.

Bigelow, Bill, and Bob Peterson. 2003. *Rethinking Columbus: The Next 500 Years*. Milwaukee, WI: Rethinking Schools Ltd.

Bishop, Claire H., and Kurt Weise. 1939. *The Five Chinese Brothers*. New York: Sandcastle.

Braschi, Giannina. 2011. *Yo-Yo Boing!* Seattle, WA: AmazonCrossing.

Callahan, Rebecca. 2006. "The Intersection of Accountability and Language: Can Reading Intervention Replace English Language Development?" *Bilingual Research Journal* 3 (1): 1–21.

———. 2013. "The English Learner Dropout Dilemma: Multiple Risks and Multiple Resources." *California Dropout Research Project Report #19*. www.cdrp.ucsb.edu/pubs_reports.htm.

Callahan, Rebecca M., and Patricia C. Gándara. 2014. *The Bilingual Advantage: Language, Literacy, and the US Labor Market*. Buffalo, NY: Multilingual Matters.

Camarota, Steven A., and Karen Zeigler. 2014. "One in Five U.S. Residents Speaks Foreign Language at Home." Center for Immigration Studies. http://cis.org/record-one-in-five-us-residents-speaks-language-other-than-english-at-home.

Carey Ryan S., Juan F. Casas, Lisa Kelly-Vance, Brigette O. Ryalls, and Collette Nero. 2010. "Parent Involvement and Views of School Success: The Role of Parents' Latino and White American Cultural Orientations." *Psychology in the Schools* 47 (4): 391–405.

Census Bureau 2010. "Population Speaking a Language Other than English at Home Increases by 140 Percent in Past Three Decades." www.census.gov/newsroom/releases/archives/american_community_survey_acs/cb10-cn58.html.

Center for Applied Linguistics. 2014. Directory of Two-Way Bilingual Immersion Programs in the U.S. www.cal.org/twi/directory/.

Chappell, Sharon, and Christian Faltis. 2006. "Spanglish, Bilingualism, Culture and Identity in Latino Children's Literature." *Children's Literature in Education* 38: 253–62.

Chimamanda Adichie. 2009. "The Danger of a Single Story". TED Talk. www.ted.com/talks/chimamanda_adichie_the_danger_of_a_single_story?language=en.

Chorney, Harold. 1997. "The Economic Benefits of Linguistic Duality and Bilingualism: A Political Economy Approach." *Official Languages and the Economy, New Canadian Perspectives* 181–94.

Collier, Virginia P., and Wayne P. Thomas. 2004. "The Astounding Effectiveness of Dual Language Education for All." *NABE Journal of Research and Practice* 2 (1): 1–20.

———. 2009. *Educating English Learners for a Transformed World*. Albuquerque, NM: Fuente Press.

———. 2012. *Dual Language Education for a Transformed World*. Albuquerque, NM: Fuente Press.

———. 2014. *Creating Dual Language Schools for a Transformed World: Administrators Speak*. Albuquerque, NM: Fuente Press.

Cortina, Regina, Carmina Makar, and Mary Faith Mount-Cors. 2015. "Dual Language as a Social Movement: Putting Languages on a Level Playing Field." *Current Issues in Comparative Education* 17 (1): 5–16.

Costa, Albert, and Nuria Sebastián-Gallés. 2014. "How Does the Bilingual Experience Sculpt the Brain?" *Nature Reviews Neuroscience* 15: 336–45.

Crawford, James. 2004. *Educating English Learners. Language Diversity in the Classroom*. Los Angeles: Bilingual Educational Services.

———. 2008. "Ten Common Fallacies About Bilingual Education." *Advocating for English Learners: Selected Essays*. Buffalo, NY: Multilingual Matters.

Cummins, James. 2001. *Negotiating Identities: Education for Empowerment in a Diverse Society*. Los Angeles: California Association for Bilingual Education.

———. 2008a. "BICS and CALP: Empirical and Theoretical Status of the Distinction." In *Encyclopedia of Language and Education. Volume 2: Literacy*, edited by Nancy H. Hornberger, 71–83. New York: Springer.

———. 2008b. "Teaching for Transfer: Challenging the Two Solitudes Assumption in Bilingual Education." In *Encyclopedia of Language and Education*, edited by Nancy Hornberger, 65–76. New York: Springer.

Cummins, James, Rania Mirza, and Saskia Stille. 2012. "Identity and Engagement: Scaffolding Learning Among Bilingual/ELL Students." *TESL Canada* 29 (6): 25–48.

de Jong, Ester J. 2004. "L2 Proficiency in a Two-Way and a Developmental Bilingual Program." *NABE Journal of Research and Practice* 2 (1): 77–108.

———. 2011. *Foundations of Multilingualism in Education: from Principles to Practice*. Philadelphia: Caslon Publishing.

de Jong, Ester J., and Carol Bearse. 2011. "The Same Outcomes for All? High School Students Reflect on Their Two-Way Immersion Program Experiences." In *Immersion Education. Practices, Policies and Possibilities,* edited by Diane J. Tedick, Donna Christian, and Tara Williams Fortune, 104–22. Buffalo, NY: Multilingual Matters.

Delaware World Language Immersion Programs. www.doe.k12.de.us/Page/1090.

Díaz, Junot. 2007. *The Brief Wondrous Life of Oscar Wao*. New York: Riverhead Books.

Directory of Two-Way Immersion Programs in the U.S. Center for Applied Linguistics. www.cal.org/twi/directory/.

Escamilla, Kathy, Susan Hopewell, and Sandra Butvilofsky. 2013. *Biliteracy from the Start: Literacy Squared in Action.* Philadelphia: Caslon Publishing.

Espinosa, Linda M. 2013. "PreK–3rd: Challenging Common Myths About Dual Language Learners." PreK-3rd Policy to Action Brief, 10. New York: Foundation for Child Development.

Ethnologue: Languages of the World, Nineteenth Edition. 2016. Dallas, TX: SIL International. www.ethnologue.com/statistics.

Fernández Vítores, David. 2015. "El Español: Una Lengua Viva. Informe 2015." Instituto Cervantes. http://eldiae.es/wp-content/uploads/2015/06/espanol_lengua-viva_20151.pdf.

Flores, Barbara M. 2005. "The Intellectual Presence of the Deficit View of Spanish-Speaking Children in the Educational Literature during the 20th Century." In *Latino Education: An Agenda for Community Action Research*, edited by Pedro Pedraza and Melissa Rivera, 75–98. New York: Routledge.

Freeman, David, and Yvonne Freeman. 2011. *Between Worlds: Access to Second Language Acquisition.* Portsmouth, NH: Heinemann.

Freeman, Yvonne, and David Freeman. 2006. *Teaching Reading and Writing in Spanish and English in Bilingual and Dual Language Classrooms.* Portsmouth, NH: Heinemann.

———. 2007. *Enseñanza de la Lectura y la Escritura en Español e Inglés: En Salones de Clases Bilingües y de Doble Inmersión.* Portsmouth, NH: Heinemann.

Gándara, Patricia C., and Rebecca M. Callahan. 2014. "Looking Toward the Future: Opportunities in a Shifting Linguistic Landscape." In *The Bilingual Advantage: Language, Literacy and the US Labor Market,* edited by Rebecca Callahan and Patricia Gándara, 286–97. Buffalo, NY: Multilingual Matters.

García, Ofelia. 2009. *Bilingual Education in the 21st Century: A Global Perspective.* New York: Wiley-Blackwell.

Genesee, Fred. 2011. "Reflecting on Possibilities for Immersion." In *Immersion Education. Practices, Policies and Possibilities,* edited by Diane J. Tedick, Donna Christian, and Tara Williams Fortune, 271–79. Buffalo, NY: Multilingual Matters.

Genesee, Fred, Kathryn Lindholm-Leary, William Saunders, and Donna Christian. 2006. *Educating English Language Learners: A Synthesis of Research Evidence.* New York: Cambridge University Press.

Giacchino-Baker, Rosalie, and Bonnie Filler. 2006. "Parental Motivation, Attitudes, Support, and Commitment in a Southern Californian Two-Way Immersion Program." *Journal of Latinos and Education* 5 (1): 5–28.

Global Competence Position Statement American Council on the Teaching of Foreign Languages. 2014. www.actfl.org/news/position-statements /global-competence-position-statement.

Goldenberg, Claude, and Rhoda Coleman. 2010. *Promoting Academic Achievement among English Learners: A Guide to the Research.* New York: Corwin.

González, Norma, Luis Moll, and Cathy Amanti. 2005. *Funds of Knowledge: Theorizing Practices in Households, Communities, and Classrooms.* Mahwah, NJ: Lawrence Erlbaum Associates.

Goulah, Jason, and Sonia Soltero. 2015. "Reshaping the Mainstream Education Climate Through Bilingual-Bicultural Education." In *Research on Preparing Inservice Teachers to Work Effectively with Emergent Bilinguals: Advances in Research in Teaching Series,* edited by Yvonne Freeman and David Freeman, 177–203. Bingley, UK: Emerald Books.

Grosjean, Francois. 2010. *Bilingual: Life and Reality.* Cambridge, MA: Harvard University Press.

Hamayan, Else, Fred Genesee, and Nancy Cloud. 2013. *Dual Language Instruction from A to Z: Practical Guidance for Teachers and Administrators.* Portsmouth, NH: Heinemann.

Harper, Candace A., and Ester J. de Jong. 2009. "English Language Teacher Expertise: The Elephant in the Room." *Language and Education* 23 (2): 127–51.

Hopewell, Susan, and Kathy Escamilla. 2014. "Biliteracy Development in Immersion Contexts." *Journal of Immersion and Content-Based Language Education* 2 (2): 181–95.

Hornberger, Nancy H. 2004. "The Continua of Biliteracy and the Bilingual Educator: Educational Linguistics in Practice." *Bilingual Education and Bilingualism* 7 (2): 155–71.

Horwitz, Elaine K. 2013. *Becoming a Language Teacher: A Practical Guide to Second Language Learning and Teaching.* Boston: Pearson.

Howard, Elizabeth R., and Julie Sugarman. 2007. *Realizing the Vision of Two-Way Immersion: Fostering Effective Programs and Classrooms.* Crystal Lake, IL: Center for Applied Linguistics and Delta Publishing Company.

Inter-American Magnet School Mission Statement. 2013. http://iamschicago.com /sites/iamschicago.com/files/Letter%20from%20Principal%207.29.13.pdf.

Jaramillo, Ann. 2008. *La Linea.* New York: Roaring Brook Press.

Jeynes, William H. 2005. "A Meta-Analysis of the Relation of Parental Involvement to Urban Elementary School Student Academic Achievement." *Urban Education* 40: 237–69.

Jiménez, Francisco. 2000. *La Mariposa.* Orlando, FL: Houghton Mifflin Harcourt.

———. 1997. *The Circuit: Stories from the Life of a Migrant Child.* Albuquerque, NM: University of New Mexico Press.

Kamwangamalu, Nikonko M. 2010. "Multilingualism and Codeswitching in Education." In *Sociolinguistics and Language Education*, edited by Nancy Hornberger and Sandra lee McKay, 116–42. Buffalo, NY: Multilingual Matters.

Krashen, Stephen. 1982. *Principles and Practice in Second Language Acquisition*. Oxford: Pergamon.

Krashen, Stephen, and Grace McField. 2005. "What Works? Reviewing the Latest Evidence on Bilingual Education." *Language Learner* 1 (2): 7–10.

Lee, Enid, Deborah Menkart, and Margo Okazawa-Rey. 2007. *Beyond Heroes and Holidays. A Practical Guide to K–12 Anti-Racist, Multicultural Education and Staff Development*. Washington, DC: Network of Educators on the Americas.

Lindholm-Leary, Kathryn. 2001. *Dual Language Education*. Buffalo, NY: Multilingual Matters.

———. 2008. "Language Development and Academic Achievement in Two-Way Immersion Programs." In *Pathways to Bilingualism: Evolving Perspectives on Immersion Education,* edited by Tara Williams Fortune and Diane J. Tedick, 177–200. Buffalo, NY: Multilingual Matters.

———. 2012. "Success and Challenges in Dual Language Education." *Theory into Practice* 51: 256–62.

———. 2014. "Bilingual and Biliteracy Skills in Young Spanish-Speaking Low-SES Children: Impact of Instructional Language and Primary Language Proficiency." *International Journal of Bilingual Education and Bilingualism* 17 (2): 144–59.

Lindholm-Leary, Kathryn and Graciela Borsato. 2005. "Hispanic High Schoolers and Mathematics: Follow-Up of Students Who Had Participated in Two-Way Bilingual Elementary Programs." *Bilingual Research Journal* 29 (3): 641–52.

———. 2006. "Academic Achievement." In *Educating English Language Learners*, edited by Fred Genesee, Kathryn Lindholm-Leary, William Saunders, and Donna Christian, 157–79. New York: Cambridge University Press.

Lindholm-Leary, Kathryn, and Ana Hernández. 2011. "Achievement and Language Proficiency of Latino Students in Dual Language Programmes: Native English Speakers, Fluent English/Previous ELLs, and Current ELLs." *Journal of Multilingual and Multicultural Development* 32: 531–45.

Logan Square Neighborhood Association. 2016. "Parent Mentor Program." www.lsna.net/Issues-and-programs/Schools-and-Youth/Parent-Mentor-Program.html.

Martin, Holly. 2005. "Code-Switching in U.S. Ethnic Literature: Multiple Perspectives Presented Through Multiple Languages." *Changing English* 12 (3): 403–15.

McLaughlin, Barry. 1992. "Myths and Misconceptions About Second Language Learning: What Every Teacher Needs to Unlearn." Educational Practice Report 5, University of California, Santa Cruz.

Memo to the Rhode Island Board of Education. 2014. http://media.ride.ri.gov/BOE/Enclosures/Enclosures_6_12_14/Encl3m_Chariho_Request_for_Amendment.pdf.

Miramontes, Ofelia B., Adel Nadeau, and Nancy L. Commins. 2011. *Restructuring Schools for Linguistic Diversity: Linking Decision Making to Effective Programs.* New York: Teachers College Press.

Mobin-Uddin, Asma. 2005. *My Name Is Bilal.* Honesdale, PA: Boyds Mills Press.

Moll, Luis C. and Norma González. 2004. "Engaging Life: A Funds of Knowledge Approach to Multicultural Education." In *Handbook of Research on Multicultural Education*, edited by James Banks and Cherry McGee Banks, 699–715. San Francisco: Jossey-Bass.

Na, An. 2003. *A Step from Heaven.* New York: Speak.

National Center for Education Statistics. 2015. "English Language Learners. The Condition of Education. Department of Education." https://nces.ed.gov/programs/coe/indicator_cgf.asp.

National Security Language Initiative for Youth. www.nsliforyouth.org/.

NYC DOE Press Release. 2015. "Chancellor Fariña to Launch 40 Dual Language Programs in September." http://schools.nyc.gov/Offices/mediarelations/NewsandSpeeches/2014-2015/Chancellor+Fari%C3%B1a+to+Launch+40+Dual+Language+Programs+in+September.htm.

Nieto, Sonia, and Patty Bode. 2012. *Affirming Diversity: The Sociopolitical Context of Multicultural Education.* Boston: Pearson

Ortiz Cofer, Judith. 1996. *An Island Like You: Stories of the Barrio.* New York: Puffin Press.

Palmer, Deborah. 2007. "A Dual Immersion Strand Programme in California: Carrying out the Promise of Dual Language Education in an English-Dominant Context." *International Journal of Bilingual Education and Bilingualism* 10 (6): 752–68.

Palmer, Deborah, and Ramón Antonio Martínez. 2013. "Teacher Agency in Bilingual Spaces: A Fresh Look at Preparing Teachers to Educate Latina/o Bilingual Children." *Review of Research in Education* 37: 269–98.

Peal, Elizabeth, and Wallace Lambert. 1962. "The Relation of Bilingualism to Intelligence." *Psychological Monographs* 76: 1–23.

Potowski, Kim. 2007. *Language and Identity in a Dual Immersion School.* Buffalo, NY: Multilingual Matters.

Rodríguez, Diane, Angela Carrasquillo, and Kung Soon Lee. 2014. *The Bilingual Advantage: Promoting Academic Development, Biliteracy, and Native Language in the Classroom.* New York: Teachers College Press.

Rodríguez, Luis. 1998 *America Is Her Name.* Evanston, IL: Curbstone Books.

Rolstad, Kellie, Kate Mahoney, and Gene Glass. 2005. "The Big Picture: A Meta-Analysis of Program Effectiveness Research on English Language Learners." *Educational Policy* 19 (4): 572–94.

Ronfeldt, Matthew, Susanna Loeb, and James Wyckoff. 2013. "How Teacher Turnover Harms Student Achievement." *American Educational Research Journal* 50 (1): 4–36.

Ryan, Camille. 2013. "Language Use in the United States: 2011." American Community Survey Reports. U.S. Department of Commerce Economics and Statistics Administration. U.S. Census Bureau. www.census.gov/prod/2013pubs/acs-22.pdf.

Saunders, William M., and Claude Goldenberg. 2007. "The Effects of an Instructional Conversation on English Language Learners' Concepts of Friendship and Story Comprehension." In *Talking Texts: How Speech and Writing Interact in School Learning,* edited by Rosalind Horowitz, 221–52. Mahwah, NJ: Erlbaum.

Saunders, William, Claude Goldenberg, and David Marcelletti. 2013. "English Language Development Guidelines for Instruction." *American Educator* 37 (2): 13–39.

Scanlan, Martin, and Francesca A. López. 2015. *Leadership for Culturally and Linguistically Responsive Schools.* New York: Routledge.

Seeger, Pete. 1998. *Abiyoyo.* New York: Aladdin.

Shin, Fay H. 2000. "Parent Attitudes Toward the Principles of Bilingual Education and Their Children's Participation in Bilingual Programs." *Journal of Intercultural Studies* 21 (1): 93–99.

Shin, Sarah J. 2013. *Bilingualism in School and Society: Language, Identity and Policy.* New York: Routledge.

Slavin, Robert, and Allan Cheung. 2003. "Effective Reading Programs for English Language Learners. A Best-Evidence Synthesis." CRESPAR Report. Johns Hopkins University, Baltimore, MD.

Sleeter, Christine E., and Carl A. Grant. 2009. *Making Choices for Multicultural Education: Five Approaches to Race, Class, and Gender.* New York: John Wiley & Sons.

Soltero, Sonia W. 2004. *Dual Language: Teaching and Learning in Two Languages.* Boston: Allyn and Bacon/Longman.

———. 2011. *Schoolwide Approaches to Educating ELLs: Creating Linguistically and Culturally Responsive K–12 Schools.* Portsmouth, NH: Heinemann.

Soltero, Sonia W., and José Soltero. 2010. "Latinos and Education in the Chicago Metropolitan Area." In *Latinos in Chicago: Reflections of an American Landscape,* edited by John Koval, 67–124. Notre Dame, IN: Institute for Latino Studies, University of Notre Dame Press.

Swain, Merrill. 1985. "Communicative Competence: Some Roles of Comprehensible Input and Comprehensible Output in its Development." In *Input in Second Language Acquisition*, edited by Susan Gass and Carolyn Madden, 235–53. Rowley, MA: Newbury House.

Tedick, Diane J., Donna Christian, and Tara Williams Fortune. 2011. "The Future of Immersion Education: An Invitation to Dwell in Possibilities." In *Immersion Education: Practices, Policies and Possibilities,* edited by Diane J. Tedick, Donna Christian, and Tara Williams Fortune, 1–10. Buffalo, NY: Multilingual Matters.

Thomas, Wayne, and Virginia Collier. 2012. "English Learners in North Carolina Dual Language Programs: Year 3 of this Study: School Year 2009–2010." http://gled.ncdpi.wikispaces.net/file/view/NCDPI%20Year%203%20exec%20 summary_FINAL.pdf/531275062/NCDPI%20Year%203%20exec%20summary _FINAL.pdf.

Utah Language Roadmap for the 21st Century. 2015. www.schools.utah.gov/CURR /dualimmersion/Home/UtahLanguageRoadmap.aspx.

Valdés, Guadalupe. 1997. "Dual-Language Immersion Programs: A Cautionary Note Concerning the Education of Language-Minority Students." *Harvard Educational Review* 67: 391–429.

Vygotsky, Lev. 1978. *Mind in Society: The Development of Higher Psychological Processes.* Cambridge, MA: Harvard University Press.

Wagner, Susan, and Tamara King. 2013. *Implementing Effective Instruction for English Language Learners: 12 Key Practices for Administrators, Teachers, and Leadership Teams.* Philadelphia: Caslon Publishing.

Wilkes, Sybella. 2004. *One Day We Had to Run! Refugee Children Tell Their Stories in Words and Paintings.* London, England: Evans Brothers Ltd.

Williams, Cen. 1996. "Secondary Education: Teaching in the Bilingual Situation." In *The Language Policy: Taking Stock*, edited by Cen Williams, Gwyn Lewis, and Colin Baker. Wales: Llangefni.

Wright, Wayne E. 2015. *Foundations for Teaching English Language Learners: Research, Theory, Policy, and Practice.* Philadelphia: Caslon Publishing.

INDEX